BEHIND THE LINES, NO. 3

Great Irish Sports Stories from *The42*, 2019

Praise for previous editions of Behind the Lines

'In these pages, the men and women of *The42* show once more why they are the nation's best and most essential sports storytellers. Irish writers are as important as Irish games, and here at the intersection is something essential.' — Wright Thompson, ESPN senior writer

'A smashing, smashing book... Full credit to *The42* for heralding their journalism and for holding up these young sportswriters so that we can all get a closer look at them.' — Paul Kimmage

'As compelling as it is often amusing and touching. These are stories that go far beyond sport, and they still resonate long after they have been read.' — Donald McRae, The Guardian

'This is storytelling at its most Irish and most eloquent.' — Dave Hannigan, author of Boy Wonder: Tales from the Sidelines of an Irish Childhood

'More evidence that terrific sports writing is just terrific writing, period... The men and women writing for *The42* provide an essential voice that speaks a universal language.' — Glenn Stout, series editor of The Best American Sports Writing

'A cracking book.' — Matt Cooper

Behind the Lines

NO. 3

- - - - - - - - - - - - - - -

Great Irish Sports Stories
from *The42*, 2019

—

JOURNAL MEDIA

Journal Media Ltd
Golden Lane
Dublin 2, Ireland.
www.the42.ie

© Journal Media 2019
ISBN 978-1-9998774-2-2
Designed by www.grahamthew.com
Edited by Adrian Russell and Niall Kelly
Printed by Scandbook AB, Sweden
This book is typeset in 10.5pt on 15pt Sabon

The paper used in this book comes from the wood pulp of managed forests. For every tree felled, at least one tree is planted, thereby renewing natural resources.

5 4 3 2 1

CONTENTS

We've spent a lot of this year speaking to some of our favourite journalists about sportswriting.

Our Behind the Lines podcast (we didn't expend too much imagination on the name) has allowed us to enjoy the company of the trade's best as they deconstruct features, interviews and books which influenced, surprised or moved them.

Like taking apart a wrist watch and putting it back together again, the process brings new appreciation for the reasons these pieces tick. But most of all, they're hugely enjoyable conversations and we learn about work which we may not have consumed previously.

Since you ask, The Unfortunates would be my first selection, should I ever be invited to appear as a guest alongside presenter Gavin Cooney.

BS Johnson's experimental novel was published in 1969. A postmodern author and hipster football writer before the term was coined, Johnson was outwardly successful and well-known in his time. Since he killed himself at 40 years of age however, he has been largely, sadly overlooked somewhat — apart from amongst collectors and academics, perhaps.

In fact, though a leading literary figure in his day, Johnson had to supplement his cheques from London publishers by working as a football reporter for the Observer newspaper, sitting in the press box each Saturday afternoon covering Division 1 and 2 games.

His editor — who I can picture as a kindred spirit, browbeaten behind a desk and in a loosened necktie — must have known he had a fiction writer and not a reporter on his hands when he picked up the phone one weekend. Johnson, at a provincial football ground during the dying minutes of a game, asked quickly: 'I've just thought of an idea for a novel. Can you take a report from the wires?'

It was on one of these assignments when the idea for a 'book in a box' came to Johnson, who arrived in Nottingham for a routine reporting job.

'When you are going away to report on soccer in a different city each Saturday,' he later wrote, 'you get the mechanics of travelling to and finding your way about in a strange place to an almost automatic state.'

As he stepped from the main railway station, he didn't therefore at first realise it was a town, yet to be touched by Brian Clough's charisma, that he'd been in many times before. He had in fact visited a good friend, Tony, there throughout his treatment, before his death from cancer.

As Johnson sat on the press benches at the City Ground by the River Trent, memories of his relationship with his old friend punctuated passages of play on the pitch. Recollections of a promise he made to write his testimony — 'I'll get it all down, mate' — and other snapshots, offered a filter through which he watched the humdrum tie play out.

The Unfortunates, made up of 27 bound chapters, is Johnson's attempt to recreate this experience. The reader is encouraged to read two chapters in a particular sequence; one at the start and the other at the end. But in between the order in which you consume the story, presented in bound pamphlets, is the reader's decision.

The device insinuates the randomness of life and memory and, perhaps too, watching and writing about sport.

In this year's book — our third in the series, thanks to your support — we're invited into Eamon Dunphy's sitting room as he flashes through scenes from his life. Consistency, he warns, is the hobgoblin of the mediocre mind.

Later, we sit around Ted Walsh's kitchen table as he lays out his homespun philosophy on racing and horses, but really... a lot more than that. As someone who works in online journalism in 2019, his advice on how to give and take criticism is invaluable. We're often told — in different ways, below the line — that 'you made a stones of that ride' or 'you didn't fucken shine on him'. Ted's son Ruby, the best in the business, takes it on board.

In between those two homes, towards the start and end of the book, the theme of family life threads through stories about young footballers abroad, World Cup wins and county championship symmetry.

As Ireland's sports story played out in front of us throughout the year, these chapters were bound up by our team of talented journalists.

It takes, of course, resources to have someone like Gavin Casey ringside in June to witness Katie Taylor win a contro-versial victory over Delfine Persoon at Madison Square Garden and then rush from the airport to file the definitive reflection on the midtown scrap. This year we asked our readers to back us in a different way by becoming members of *The42*. You can imagine how surprised we were when they did.

This vibrant community now enjoy access to lovely, extra stuff like podcasts and newsletters directly from our journalists, invitations to events with us and sport's big person-alities, discounts for nice merchandise, entry for ticket draws, and most interestingly, a real voice in our newsroom through

Town Hall events and other forums. Our membership chose the cover of this book, for example.

We're excited to explore the opportunities of member-supported journalism as we enter an exciting new phase. (You can join at members.the42.ie).

In the meantime, we hope you enjoy these stories; in whichever order you choose to read them.

ADRIAN RUSSELL
Editor, The42

ONE

A STAR IN THE SKY

—

EOIN O'CALLAGHAN | 27 JANUARY

IT SAID MUCH that when Anne O'Brien died in 2016, it was international news. There was some minor coverage in the Irish media but much more detailed reporting in other countries.

In Italy, various outlets paid tribute. One Lazio site prefaced the news with 'one of our eagles has flown to heaven'. In Trani, the southern fishing town where she won a Scudetto and an Italian Cup, a local journalist, Franco Caffarella, was emotional as he described her talents.

'She had class and she had vision,' he said. 'She was a pure talent who illuminated Italian women's football. Now she's a star in the sky.'

Her death was heavily covered in Sweden too.

At the time, Pia Sundhage — an iconic figure in the women's game who was in charge of the US side between 2008 and 2012 — was manager of the Swedish national team. She and Anne had met in the mid-80s, when Sundhage spent a season with Lazio. She was stunned when informed of her former team-mate's passing.

'Has she gone? I had no idea,' she said.

'She wasn't so much older than I am. Oh, my God. I didn't know. We actually lived together for a while — five girls in an apartment. Anne was friendly, helpful and always had a smile on her face. Before I learned Italian, I spoke some English so it was pretty easy to talk to her. She was always helpful in translating from Italian when our trainer Sergio Guenza spoke so quickly! She was the kind of midfielder that ran and ran and ran. But she had great technique too. She was quick and always worked for everyone else.'

She'd been in Italy for four decades, her journey an inexplicable and remarkable one.

'She started playing football from a very young age, on the road in Inchicore,' says Tony O'Brien, Anne's brother.

'She was about 14 when she played for a team called Julian Vards and they played out of Donore Avenue or around that area. She got her first football boots around that time, when my mam finally gave in and bought her a pair.

'After that, she joined the All-Stars who were based in Ballyfermot. It was a team made up of girls from all around Dublin. She won everything with them for a few years and it was through them that she was spotted, really. In the summer of 1973, she was called up to an Ireland Selection team. The game was against Stade de Reims from France who were on a tour of the country. She was only 17 at the time but afterwards they asked her to travel and play with them for the rest of the Irish tour. And after that it was all done really quickly.'

The deal was historic. No female player from Britain or Ireland had ever played professionally in Europe before.

Anne O'Brien was a revolutionary figure.

Her manager in France was Pierre Geoffroy, a revolutionary figure in his own right and who had assembled the side along with Richard Gaud in the late-60s, when there was still a ban in place preventing women from being pro footballers. It was 1970 when the authorities lifted that barrier and Gaud would later comment that despite some misogynistic remarks at the very start of the rebirth, people were amazed by the standard of play. Within a couple of years, a few thousand would turn up to championship games and the club used their new-found fame to begin touring and spreading the word.

'Geoffroy felt it was the beginning of something,' Gaud said last year, as Stade de Reims celebrated 50 years since the formation of the women's team.

'But it was the players who really took their destiny into their own hands, they wanted something and they did it. What was basically just entertainment became the beginning of a beautiful story.'

Anne was a crucial part of the narrative. Bowing to her mother's demands, she waited until she turned 18 before moving to the north-western city, about 90 minutes' drive from Paris. She was big news but seemed completely unfazed by both the move and the attention.

'She was in all the papers,' Tony says.

'It was on the news over here but then she was on ITN in London and obviously it was all covered in the French newspapers too. It was huge.'

In one pun-heavy report from March 1974 ('Anne, belle of the ball'), she was described as the team's 'goalscoring sensation', earning a reported £100 per week and with 'fringe benefits like a glass of champagne before each match, and another at half-time — just to add a sparkle to the game'.

'I started playing when I was two years old — as soon as I could walk,' she told reporter Michael Brown, who watched her score against nearby Mourmelon the previous day.

'I left my boyfriend behind to take this big chance and they have been wonderfully friendly and kind.'

Her impact on the team was immediate and she would win three successive French championships between 1974 and 1976. Her performances were so impressive that she was selected for a French League XI for a game against a Rest of Europe side at the end of her debut campaign.

'My ma was in France with her and there are lovely photos of the two of them walking the streets of Paris together,' Tony says.

'She was after winning the French Cup and was after scoring a hat-trick in that game.

'Her face was all over the billboards. They called her 'Nanou', a nickname that was probably derived from Anne. And there were trips all over the world to play games too. She was in places like Guadeloupe and Haiti and those matches were watched by thousands of fans.'

Back in Dublin, the family didn't carry much worry or anxiety. They felt it was Anne's destiny of sorts.

'She always knew she'd end up in football,' Tony says.

'She never wanted to do anything else. In those days, you got on with it no matter what you did. People went on their different journeys all over the world. Everything was pretty straightforward and off she went to France. But we knew Anne and that it would be her for the rest of her life. Because football was her life. It was all she did and all she ever wanted to do.'

In 1976, history repeated itself. Stade de Reims went on a

tour to Italy at the end of the season and Anne quickly became a transfer target for Lazio. Their offer of full-time football was too good to turn down so, still aged just 20, she headed for Rome.

'The money was much better in Italy,' Tony says. 'She was always happy there because it was Rome and she loved it. That was her home, really.'

At the end of her first season in the capital, she picked up a Coppa Italia medal after Lazio beat the reigning champions Milan in a shootout. And in 1979, she was a league winner as the Biancocelesti claimed the Scudetto for the first time. The following year, they did it again.

Anne was a classic number 10 and part of an immensely talented side that also boasted the prolific Danish striker Susanne Augustesen and distinguished defender Maura Furlotti.

'I would've been over a lot to watch her and it was brilliant,' Tony says.

'The matches were packed out and the way they did it over there was that if it was a big game like the semi-final of the cup, they'd have the women on before a men's fixture so everyone would be in the ground and it would nearly be full capacity for the last part of the women's match.

'It was brilliant to be there and to see her on the pitch. I know she was my sister but, my Jesus, she was a brilliant player. She was way better than half of them over in Italy. She nursed the ball and she fed the ball. She fed everyone everything. A great passer, great control, great technique. Brilliant at taking the ball down from the air. Dribbling. Crossing for the forwards. Then, bang! Back of the net! And isn't it a pity that we don't have any videos of her playing? There might be something out there but it's probably like trying to find a needle in a haystack. There could have been a fella taping a men's game who caught the final few minutes of a women's fixture. But maybe we'll never know.'

During the 1982/83 season, Anne was persuaded to leave Rome and headed for the west coast along with Augustesen to sign for seaside club Trani. She certainly had excellent timing because despite ending the season as runners-up, the side still claimed an Italian Cup before returning in 1984 and winning the championship. It was Anne's third Scudetto in eight years.

She did return to Lazio briefly and racked up another Coppa Italia while she was there but despite inching towards her 30s, she remained in demand. There were stints in Modena, Napoli and Prato and while at the former, she gave birth to a son, Andrea.

'She was back playing straightaway,' Tony says.

'I'm sure it was four weeks later that she was playing for the team again. And she used to breastfeed Andrea in the dressing room.'

Later, there was further success with Reggiana and Milan and when Anne finally called it a day in 1994, she'd accumulated five Scudetti with four different teams. It was an astonishing haul.

But, despite being one of the finest players in Europe for two decades, she only ever played four times for Ireland. Once she left for France in the mid-70s, it was a financial and logistical inconvenience for her to be named in squads. So, regardless of her relentless success, she was effectively ignored.

'She would always come back in the summer and every Christmas too,' Tony says.

'In conversations in the house she would talk about it. But

there was always a money element involved in those days with the Irish women's team. There was very little to go around and I'm not sure if there was even much given to the players. If I remember correctly, around 1980 there was a story about them having to pay their own way to Wales or Scotland. The trip was only subsidised and not fully covered. Anne played a lot for Ireland when she was younger and on one occasion they did fly her home for a game against the Netherlands.

'But Italy was her home. Now, she called Dublin home too but that was really her home and Andrea is still over there. Forty years of her life were spent there. It's where she died and we were all with her at the time. And it's just a pity that she didn't stay around a little bit longer...'

Anne did her coaching badges and had spells at two of her former clubs — Milan and Lazio — while she also worked with the Italian Football Federation. Later, she concentrated on coaching local youngsters close to her home by the beach in Fregene, about 40 minutes outside Rome.

The family remain immensely proud of everything Anne achieved in her life and Tony, especially, is an encyclopaedia when it comes to his sister's career. He's kept every medal, every newspaper clipping, every photograph. He reels off names and addresses that date back more than 40 years.

'She went away when she was 18 and she died at 60 — what a life,' he says.

'And the Irish girls now are at the top clubs — Arsenal, Liverpool, some are in America.

'That's great to see. It's lovely, isn't it? The world has changed for the best and it's getting better. Anne would be delighted and very proud. But she was always proud.'

TWO

ABOUT SCHMIDT

—

MURRAY KINSELLA | 23 AUGUST

THE FACT THAT Joe Schmidt has torn his hamstring several times during Ireland's warm-ups before games says a lot about how much he cares for his team and their preparation.

While most head coaches stand and observe their players getting ready for matches, Schmidt — now 53 years of age — goes gung-ho as the starting backline run through plays, their boss slotting in as an opposition wing and giving it socks.

He might not have the pace of old — pace that helped him to play for Manawatu in his younger years — but Schmidt's involvement can be genuinely motivating for his players.

'If he cares this much, I need to match that.'

It's one sign of the ceaseless intensity and passion that Schmidt brings to his work, key characteristics that have helped him to major successes with Leinster and Ireland — Heineken Cups, a Grand Slam, Six Nations titles, beating the All Blacks, and more.

The man who hails from Kawakawa at the top of New Zealand's North Island, but grew up in the sleepy little town of Woodville, tends to leave a lasting mark on the players he works with, even years on from their direct involvement.

'I still hear Joe's voice in my head, probably every day,' says the now-retired Isa Nacewa, who famously played a key role in luring Schmidt to Leinster in the first place.

'It's really weird. Even when I'm not near rugby, I genuinely hear his voice in my head at least once a day, maybe more.

'Even if I'm playing a game with my daughters and they throw me a ball, I'm thinking, 'Good players take those.' It's Joe's voice still in my head. Once you create really good habits, it's hard to break them.'

Those strong habits are a huge part of Schmidt's makeup. While his rugby intellect is a well-known and key strength, his work behind the scenes to instill good habits and create consistency in how his players prepare is just as important. Schmidt has utterly revolutionised Irish rugby in that sense.

Standards now — for players, coaches, supporters, even the media — are simply different from what existed before. The way we discuss rugby in this country has been changed by Schmidt.

'He talks about, 'We are what we do every day',' explains Kevin McLaughlin, who was coached by Schmidt at Leinster and with Ireland.

'If you're doing sloppy things like standing up at a ruck in training or going into a tackle without the extra couple of steps to get your shoulder close to contact, even when it's non-contact in training, that's going to transfer over to a missed tackle in a game or getting counter-rucked.'

McLaughlin is now director of sales and operations for Kitman Labs, and he has brought Schmidt traits — 'being tough on myself, controlling things that are controllable, getting the details right' — into his new line of work.

Nacewa, who is a financial advisor with Money Empire back in New Zealand and will also work as a World Cup analyst for Spark Sport, echoes the sentiment that Schmidt leaves a lifelong imprint on the players he works with.

He goes back to simply catching the ball as an example of how Schmidt, a teacher by trade before moving into coaching full-time, builds habits.

'Drico at one time, Johnny [Sexton], myself — there might have been a pass that wasn't a decent pass, whether it was dipping at your feet or way out in front of you. The reaction would have been, 'That was a crap pass', but he'd look at you and say, 'Good players take those',' says Nacewa, who first worked with Schmidt at the Blues in New Zealand.

'I remember doing a warm-up with tennis balls just for fun and I dropped one of them and he walked past me and said, 'Good players take those.'

'When you hear that daily, he knows how to create really good habits in his players and staff, that expectation that you don't blame something else.'

Habits breed consistency and consistency breeds success in Schmidt's world.

Another element of his non-rugby-specific coaching focus is mental skills. The current Ireland squad regularly practise mindfulness as a group, with strength and conditioning coach Jason Cowman leading the sessions.

Schmidt pushes his players to go to the 'mind gym', where they spend time sitting and working through moves and tactics mentally — ensuring they don't always have to be on their feet on the pitch to better understand their roles.

Nacewa explains that Schmidt has always been rigorous in making sure he genuinely understands mental skills himself, rather than just bringing in an expert in order to tick that box.

'I remember back in around 2006 with the Blues, even before I really grasped mental skills, there was someone due to come in and run a visualisation course,' says Nacewa.

'The guy pulled out last minute but Joe being Joe, he said, 'Don't worry, I'll take it.'

'Most of us didn't really know what visualisation was but he had done the homework and ran us through the whole session. That was actually my first taste of mental skills.'

Schmidt also has an understanding of how he can use pressure and critical feedback to bring about better and more consistent training and game-day performances from his players.

His demands for high standards simply never stop and the feedback for those who fall short can be ruthless, most famously at his squad review sessions in the days after games.

'He can be extremely cutting if you don't deliver what he expects of you,' explains McLaughlin. 'For me, that's okay because it was clear what was expected and there was no confusion.

'We had immense clarity on what was expected of us and that means the feedback is fair. That's good management.

'What really gets him peeved is someone forgetting to run around the corner on a dummy line.

'The actual play might be on the other side of the pitch but he'd pick out the tighthead prop who forgot to run around the corner on the other side of the ruck to hold one defender, as that's going to stop the fold to allow us to get an overlap. That's the kind of thing that really, really gets his goat.

'On the other hand, if we did positive things based on what was expected of us, he was really quick to let us know that was good.'

Schmidt's reviews with individual players have always been as detailed but it's something that is appreciated by those who are genuinely hungry to get better. More distance on a linekick, extra power in the pass, lower body height on clearouts — Schmidt always demands more and delivers action plans to help his players to improve.

Of course, Schmidt's time with Ireland has not been all plain-sailing. The 2015 World Cup was a very difficult experience as Ireland lost five key players for the quarter-final defeat to Argentina.

But even without their most important men, it was a poor showing from Ireland and Schmidt has perhaps learned personal lessons from that tournament. It has been very notable that the current pre-season has been a far more relaxed affair than last time around, with Ireland mixing up their training locations and giving players intermittent time off.

For Schmidt, switching off from rugby is perhaps the greatest challenge.

'I'd say that's one really hard thing for him to do,' says Nacewa. 'I genuinely think he probably has to schedule those days that he can switch off into the year and weeks.

'He does a lot with Luke, his son, then a lot of charity work, and that might be the time he gets that balance to switch off. He gives talks at schools and clubs, and that might balance him so he cannot think about rugby for a second.'

One thing that has always surprised journalists is how much time Schmidt invests in keeping up to date on what's being said and written in the media — certainly not a controllable factor.

Obviously, the wider perception of Ireland and his work is important but it's likely another of the key challenges for Schmidt as a coach — trying not to get worked up by opinions he doesn't agree with.

But really the sheer intensity of his character is a strength. His incessant desire to be better prepared drives his Ireland team, and did so with Leinster before that.

'He's a complete professor of the game and, to be honest, I had very few conversations with him that weren't either directly about or related to rugby,' says McLaughlin. 'I was totally okay with that, it was my job and I liked the intensity he brought.

'Most coaches are quite obsessed with rugby but he was the most I've ever seen. It's pretty incredible — you're talking to him and he remembers a specific moment you were involved in from the season before.

'You're thinking, 'Jeez, if he remembers that from a year ago, imagine what he remembers from the game I just played, I better get my shit together.' It's about making sure lads are always on their toes, never resting on their laurels.'

Nacewa and Schmidt have a closer relationship than most of his players would, given that they first worked together back in New Zealand and then the fact that Nacewa provided the link to Leinster, ensuring the Joe era actually got underway.

Nacewa knows the intense side of his former head coach, but also the personal touches.

'He works so hard, studies so hard and is meticulous in his planning of everything — whether that's travel times, tactics, training — everyone knows his rugby mind and the amount of hours of footage he watches.

'But if you take him away from rugby for a bit, which is hard to do, he's so down-to-earth. He will help out anyone who asks and if you're lucky enough to get him away from rugby, he's good to sit down with for a conversation as a mate. I cherish those conversations.

'If you need help in any aspect of life, he'll pick up the phone as soon as you walk away and make a few calls, help out, and he wouldn't want any credit for it whatsoever.

'He's a really genuine guy at the end of the day. That reflects through Kellie, his wife, and all of his family. They're down-to-earth people with really good values.

'In my eyes, what he enjoys the most about his work is the players celebrating with partners and their families at the end of a win.

'Now, the real great champions don't celebrate for long. You might celebrate for two, three, four, five days — depending on your age — but you're straight back thinking about what's next.

'Joe relaxes for hours rather than days but when he sees players with their kids and parents and families, he cherishes that the most.'

Whatever happens in the coming months in Japan, there is little doubt that Schmidt will leave a lasting mark on Irish rugby when he steps down to make way for Andy Farrell.

Schmidt will prioritise his family thereafter but most who have come across the man have a feeling that he won't stay away from rugby for too long. If he does finish with this World Cup, the game will be worse off without him.

THREE

THE HOBGOBLIN OF
THE MEDIOCRE MIND

—

GAVIN COONEY | 23 FEBRUARY

'FUCK YESTERDAY.

'I can't stand old guys reminiscing about yesterday, and how great it fucking was.

'I can't stand that shit.'

By that stage, *The42* had already spent the morning muddying Eamon Dunphy's front room with an excavation of one of the most famous careers in modern Irish public life.

* * *

The42 arrived around 90 minutes earlier.

Dunphy is sitting at a desk behind a laptop with phone in hand, contemplating Ireland's prospects under Mick McCarthy with the other person down the line. He gestures toward the couch, and apologises for the delay.

The television in front of him — pulled closer into focus — is showing (a happily muted) Leaders' Questions. The day's papers are strewn about Dunphy's feet, with a wall of shelves behind him heaving with hundreds of books.

Behind the television showing politics and toward the bottom of a small stack of DVDs is a boxset of the BBC's classic political satire The Thick of It. Beside this stack is a small pile of books pulled separate from the shelving. Two of Dunphy's books — his memoirs and his biography of Matt Busby — are among them.

Once off the phone he apologises again, stressing how busy he is.

Dunphy's latest guise is the man behind a successful media start-up: his podcast The Stand attracts a six-figure listenership every week and has Tesco Finest on board as a sponsor.

There are at least five new episodes a week: football discussions with John Giles, Liam Brady and Didi Hamann go alongside analyses of front-page issues.

The scattered newspapers testify to his doing all of the podcast's research himself, and he rifles through his considerable contacts book to arrange guests. He then presents the show and sits in on the edit.

While the workload is heavy, you might not be surprised to hear that Dunphy is enjoying being his own boss.

'I am fascinated, and I want to work. It is better to work for yourself in journalism these days, because you have control over the product.'

Control… and space.

'Journalism is not in its golden age in Ireland. The podcast allows you to be independent, it allows you to get away from soundbites, it is long-form journalism.'

The podcast is the closest thing he has had to The Last Word on Today FM, the radio show he namechecks along with his biography of Matt Busby as his best work.

In spite of a hectic schedule, Dunphy is generous in making time for *The42*. Particularly as we've come armed with a series of 'Remember Whens'.

* * *

'Two years ago, I decided not to renew my contract with RTÉ Sport. At the time, they prevailed upon me to stay and, in fact, offered me a rise, a small one, to do so.

'However, before the World Cup I told them this time, I would be leaving.'

– Eamon Dunphy, July 2018

Seven months on, does he miss RTÉ?

'No. Not at all.'

Did he watch their coverage of Liverpool against Bayern Munich on Tuesday night?

'I watched the match itself on BT. But I watched the panel, such as it is now, on RTÉ.'

Does he have an opinion on it?

'Well, they're fine, Liam was working. But they've changed it. It's, kind of... we'll have to see if people like it.'

How have they changed it?

'Well if you don't have Liam and Didi and John and Bill and myself, you've changed it. They have no time at all after the match, they have to be off-air, and they have no highlights of other games or any of that.

'It's a new... paradigm I think they call it, and there are

loads of ads. Jesus, look at half-time.'

Why didn't he want to have any part of this new paradigm?

'It was dumbing down. And they have been dumbing down for years, in a big way.'

How was it being dumbed down? *The42* noted the introduction of an interactive tactics screen in the middle of the studio in recent years.

'It was second-hand and didn't always work. It was a terrifying experience for most of the panel to go and stand behind this thing that only worked some of the time.

'They could have got [Graeme] Souness back, but they didn't. They passed. They could have got Neil Lennon, but they didn't.

'I was there 40 years and I used to be friendly with the Head of Sport. There used to be mutual respect: you'd suggest something, they would suggest something, and then something would be agreed.

'But when it came to Souness I tried and when it came to Lennon I tried, but they didn't... I didn't have a voice anymore.

'Slowly it just... yeah.'

Did he feel disrespected?

'I wasn't disrespected. I was ignored. I told them if you go there you'll get what you need, and if you don't you won't. So they didn't go there... and I went home.'

He breaks into laughter.

Is *The42*'s inkling that he didn't enjoy punditry as much after John Giles finished up after Euro 2016 a fair one?

'No, no. We obviously missed John as he is the best, but Liam and Didi, fine. Really top-class players and top-class analysts. No one better, nowhere better.

'That's what you want.

'Souness, I wish we got back, as he was very, very good. That's what you want to work on: programmes that are as good as they can be, rather than chucking any old body in there. And that was evident if you were to go forensically through the last few major championships.

'There were all sorts.

'Kenny Cunningham [he puts his head in hands]... for fuck's sake.'

When John Giles was surprisingly uninvolved with the RTÉ panel for the Euro 2016 qualifier between Ireland and Scotland, RTÉ's then Head of Sport Ryle Nugent said that he was preparing the public for a life beyond the panel, believing the 'audience, subconsciously, doesn't like change... all the research would show it's [best to have] gradual rather than absolute change'.

Did Eamon agree?

'I totally agreed with that project. But there were people they could have got that they didn't.

'Lee Carsley is a former Irish international and he is doing brilliant coaching work with the FA. We could have got him. We didn't even fucking ring him.'

Has RTÉ been left behind?

'Yes.'

Left behind by the football coverage on Virgin Media?

'Souness is outstanding, Neil Lennon is very good and Brian Kerr is good. The rest of them are no good.'

What about Niall Quinn?

'No. For fuck's sake.'

* * *

'Where was the outrage when the impact of Aviva debt forced the FAI to make staff redundant? The outrage when regional development officers were told their jobs no longer existed, or would face pay cuts they are still trying to restore?

'What about Delaney's salary? The governance of the League of Ireland? The curious stewarding of sections in the Aviva Stadium that are critical of the FAI? The survival of the same faces in the boardroom, with age and term limits, pushed out to prolong their stay?

'The old Dunphy would have been all over that. But when a strong voice was required, he was pitifully weak.

'A man that used to generate serious debate on the direction of Irish football had become an obstacle to it.'

– Daniel McDonnell, IRISH INDEPENDENT, *July 2018*

Amid the profusion of tributes, the 'Best Moment' listicles and the Rod Liddle memes upon Dunphy's RTÉ departure, an Irish Independent article headlined 'Eamon Dunphy had become an obstacle for serious debate on Irish football and he will not be missed' stood out.

Dunphy hadn't read it — or at least hadn't read the above excerpt.

Is it fair?

'I think he is quite right to point out that these things happened and there was nothing as a TV analyst you could do about it. We weren't working journalists, we weren't reporters. When I was working for the Sunday Independent back in the day, I would have addressed those things.'

Why was there nothing he could do as a TV analyst about it?

'Post an international game it would be off-subject.'

Would it really have been off-subject?

'If I had been the editor we would have done it. But I wasn't. That's the problem.'

So is it fair to say that RTÉ prevented him from talking about these bigger issues regarding the FAI?

'No, that wouldn't be fair to RTÉ. These are issues that need to be done ideally by a newspaper, or in a special programme focusing on the FAI. So you need to commission that programme for TV.

'But in a post-match analysis situation, it wouldn't be much good talking about the politicking of the FAI, if you follow me.'

Nope, not really.

'We were employed to do analysis of an international match. You could argue that these things might have fed into the performance of the international team, which I don't think is right.

'I have no problem with being criticised by a young gun for not raising those things. My defence would be that first of all, when I was working at the Sunday Independent, I did a lot of stuff critical of the FAI and I was critical of a lot of other stuff.

'But I wasn't doing that. I wasn't a reporter, if you follow me.

'I would say it is fair to say I didn't do those things, because I didn't, and it is fair to say that the old Dunphy would have addressed those things. That's fair.

'Where it breaks down is that I was a barrier to them being said on RTÉ. I don't get that. I didn't have the power to edit the programme. I couldn't go into RTÉ on a Monday and say, 'Right, there's a match on Wednesday and we are going to deal with all of these things.'

'Someone else was doing that in there.

'There is a power thing there. For example, he could say that Dunphy didn't address these things on his podcast. But I couldn't on RTÉ because I had no power.

'I couldn't even get Souness back!

'Since leaving the Sunday Indo, and doing The Last Word, I've primarily been a broadcaster. Most of the time, apart from The Last Word and before the podcast, I was a broadcaster working on someone else's programme.

'They called the editorial line. It wasn't that I wilfully ignored that, it's that I felt the torch may have been passed to the other guys. The younger guys.'

Is the assertion that there is an 'Old Dunphy', and by logic a 'New Dunphy', fair?

'Yeah, that's fair. I don't mind that.'

Is the difference that one held the pen, while the other was on TV and no longer throwing it?

'Yes.

'What you can do with the pen, first of all, you can research that and you can go to the press conferences and challenge and ask questions, and then you can say 'this isn't happening' and you can write that piece week after week.

'You have to persist.

'I had been out of the persisting game for 20 years.'

Does he miss being the firebrand with the 'crazy pen', to quote a phrase he used in his memoirs?

'The fiery guy hasn't gone: the platforms have altered. You could get on the podcast and talk fire and fury for 40 minutes but the listeners will be gone. You are facilitating people to tell their stories, it is a different thing.

'Everyone who is looked at closely enough over the space of 40 years, you will spot inconsistencies. That's something that is thrown at me and it is fair enough.

'People are entitled to their point of view.'

And inconsistencies aren't necessarily a bad thing, generally speaking?

'Consistencies are the hobgoblin of the mediocre mind.'

* * *

'Notoriety itself didn't really bother me. But I felt remorse for the collateral damage inflicted on my family. On the night of the Homecoming, with the country in carnival mode, my seventeen-year-old son Tim was roughed up at a disco. He was a lovely, popular boy.

'Now Tim was the son of 'that bastard' Dunphy. My daughter Colette had been getting serious grief at school and round the neighbourhood. I had become an embarrassment to my family. I was running away to France while they dealt with the consequences of having a dad who seemed to many of their friends and neighbours to be an attention-seeking freak.'

– *Eamon Dunphy,* THE ROCKY ROAD, 2013

'It was fucking desperate', remembers Dunphy of the reaction to his criticism of Jack Charlton during Italia '90. While he was corralled by fans in Italy and subjected to chants of 'If you hate fucking Dunphy clap your hands' the flak was dished out with profligacy, and some of it hit his children.

How does he reflect on it now?

'When you see your own children suffering... a good

question would be if I'd do it again.'

Would he do it again?

'I was so fucking insensitive and so wrapped up in this journalism that I put my own kids at risk. That's a wake-up call. When I realised that, I thought 'Jesus… I shouldn't be doing that'. No job is worth that.

'But I was so… engaged by the work I was doing and that may be the nature of doing it properly, or to the level I did it.

'You kind of… lose the plot. If it's more important for you to get your story in the paper and say what you want to say, and then have your kids bullied on the street, then there's something wrong with you.

'That's on me.'

* * *

'The ideal Ireland that we would have, the Ireland that we dreamed of, would be the home of a people who valued material wealth only as a basis for right living, of a people who, satisfied with frugal comfort, devoted their leisure to the things of the spirit — a land whose countryside would be bright with cosy homesteads, whose fields and villages would be joyous with the sounds of industry, with the romping of sturdy children, the contest of athletic youths and the laughter of happy maidens, whose firesides would be forums for the wisdom of serene old age.'

  – *Eamon de Valera*, 'THE IRELAND THAT WE DREAMED OF',
March 1943

'A country that trains nurses and can't keep them. A country that has, tonight, in emergency accommodation, children who have to get up at six o'clock tomorrow morning, get a bus for an hour, go to school, walk the streets, come back to the bed and breakfast. The trolleys: 590,000 on a hospital waiting list. What on earth did we fight for our freedom for? To live in a kip like this?'

- *Eamon Dunphy,* THE TONIGHT SHOW, *September 2017*

Eamon Dunphy is named after de Valera, owing to his mother's political affiliations. The comparisons end there: I doubt that de Valera's utopian 'sounds of industry' had room for the trappings of showbiz, baby.

If he were alive today, what would Dev think of Dunphy?

'I don't think he would have thought of an Eamon Dunphy, who was a football commentator and a fairly mediocre Millwall footballer! I'm sure he would have disapproved. All of those disapprove. All of the suits.'

Whereas the suits knew only corridors, Dunphy knew the streets.

He grew up in a working-class family in Drumcondra, and when he was nine, he and his family came close to losing their home. In December 1954, the banks of the Tolka burst and flooded the lower half of Dunphy's one-up-one-down home. Living upstairs, the Dunphys weren't affected, but when the lower half was destroyed the landlord tried to move them out. Dunphy's mother fought into the Four Courts and won a battle that resonates with him

Sixty-five years on.

Given all that has changed in his life, does Dunphy still identify as working class?

'Yes. Very much so. I have an empathy and an experience

that is working class and I identify with those people, whether it is through sports commentary or social affairs politics. I understand what it is to be poor, to be homeless, to worry about where the next meal is or whether you'll have a job next week.

'All of these things are pressing concerns for a majority of people in Ireland. And if you don't understand these things, and don't have an empathy for people, you aren't likely to be very good at your job, be it in politics or journalism.'

* * *

'He's a terrible player. He can't run, he can't pass, he can't tackle, he doesn't see anything. He drives two Ferraris; I think he's a very lucky lad to have 50 caps for Ireland.'

- Eamon Dunphy, September 2013

'I'm a footballer but I'm a normal person away from the pitch. But like I said, certain stuff did get a little bit personal. I think my background was brought up and there was a thing written about a car I was driving, which was mentioned.

'And I definitely didn't drive that car.'

- Glenn Whelan, November 2018

Where was Dunphy's empathy for Glenn Whelan, the quintessential 'good pro' to whom he dedicated Only A Game?

'I accept the point you're making and you'd have to be arrogant or hard to say, 'Fuck Glenn Whelan and his family, I don't care'.

'I do care, of course I care. I would go so far as saying that maybe I went on about it too much, but every game I saw I thought, 'What's he doing?''

'That's hard to square when you talk about empathy. He is a working class boy, he has done really well, someone I'm sure I'd like, but if you are working for the fans, which I was, for the people who love the game, I think you have to be honest with them.

"This is what I think about this guy.'

"The team isn't functioning and this is the reason why.'

'And that can be hard.

'If you said to me, would you have liked to have earned the caps that Glenn Whelan earned, have had the number of Premier League appearances he had and the opportunities that go with that, would you take it and let him sit there and slag you?

'I'd take it.'

Is it a money thing? Is he jealous of how well-paid the 'good pro' is today?

'No. I want them to get more. No! I wish they were getting more! I fucking love seeing players on private jets. No! After all the things we see: Gordon Banks had to sell his memorabilia; Nobby Stiles is sick and penniless.

'No! Not at all.'

* * *

"Remember when' is the lowest form of conversation.'

- Tony Soprano

Dunphy says he hasn't seen The Sopranos but agrees with the sentiment.

However, he does recount a couple of meetings from the past.

He recalls having dinner with Don King in Las Vegas — 'He was a really bad man. It was amazing' — and meeting Stanley Matthews — 'a very dignified, intelligent, cultured man. And he was from Stoke, which is the arsehole of England.'

He remembers meeting Muhammad Ali at an Amnesty International event with U2, describing the boxer as 'the most extraordinary man in every respect'.

'A great hero. If you ever tried to measure yourself against him you quickly realise, 'I'm a long way from here'.

'That is the thing you have to remember. There have been great, great people who have left great legacies. And gifted. Ali was the first person in the public eye in the US to take against the Vietnam War, and refuse the draft.

'He got suspended and threatened with prison. He was the first prominent American to publicly reject the Vietnam War. These are heroes.'

We now live in an age, says Dunphy, in which 'the clothes of a lot of the great campaigners for social justice have been stolen by a whole army of chancers'.

'If you're talking about Ali, Martin Luther King, Bobby Kennedy, all of a sudden you then realise, 'Fuck me, Donald Trump is sitting where JFK sat'.

'Fuck. Me.

'That is a mind-fucking-blower. That's where we have come to.'

In a recent interview with Dion Fanning of JOE, Dunphy revealed that his feted biography of Matt Busby — 'the best thing I did by a million miles' — is out of print.

Talk turns to the idea of his own legacy. If the work of which he is most proud proves transient and ephemeral, does he give much thought to what he will leave behind?

'Only in terms of my family. I am very much not impressed by the idea that what I do is important. What doctors and nurses do is important; what mothers do is important, what a father does is important.

'I really don't think that being a football analyst or a journalist contributes very much, except that you might add slightly to the... gaiety of the nation.

'I don't have any notions about myself and my place in the world, which is why I have an outrageous sense of humour and I can take the piss out of myself. I think if you think about that sort of thing, you're off the wall.

'Be normal, be human, and enjoy the day you are there.

'And although it gets me into trouble — say what you think, don't be ducking and diving.'

Dunphy is too busy to indulge any more of our sepia.

Along with the podcast, he is continuing to work on the second volume of his memoirs, and is remaining loyal to the title Wrong About Everything.

'You have to keep perspective. The most important thing in life is to keep perspective.

"Who am I, and where am I in the greater scheme of things?"

'The answer is I'm a small guy in a small town, working away.

'That's it.'

* * *

There may be an old Dunphy, a new Dunphy, and a newer Dunphy still... but there is always a Dunphy.

Hence the governing principle of staying alive for more than 73-and-a-half years, baby.

Fuck yesterday.

FOUR

HALF THE WORLD AWAY

—

SINÉAD FARRELL | 30 MARCH

WHEN CLARE DUAL star Ailish Considine first relocated to Australia to pursue her Aussie Rules dream, her mother made her a promise.

Considine had signed a deal with the Adelaide Crows club for the AFLW season after impressing at an international camp, and she was eager for her mother Kay to come out for a visit.

It's a long way from West Clare to Adelaide, and initially, Kay was reluctant to make the journey.

But Ailish was persistent. And as time went on, all the signs were indicating that the Kilmihil woman would be booking a flight to Australia.

'I said, 'Look if you get to the final, I'll go out,' never even thinking she'd get a game,' Kay thought to herself at the outset of her daughter's AFLW adventure.

'The Crows wanted to fly us out at Christmas time but Ailish came home instead and I said, 'Oh my God, I wouldn't be able for that journey, not at my age.'

'And then a few weeks ago, a neighbour who would be good friends with my mother and is in his 80s, he flew out to Adelaide.

'He lived in Australia for a lot of his life and he met up with Ailish in Adelaide. So, she said, 'If he can fly at 84, you can fly," she laughs.

On the night she speaks to *The42*, Kay is making the final preparations for that trip she didn't think would ever happen.

She's quick to stress that she 'doesn't like the limelight' but within seconds of answering the call, she's at ease while talking about her accomplished daughter. The sports gene is strong in the Considine household but Kay's modest tone belies the talent among her children.

In addition to Ailish's exploits in Australia, her other daughter Eimear is an Irish international rugby player who previously won an All-Ireland intermediate title with the Clare ladies footballers.

And while Kay appreciates that results and silverware are important to her kids, their safety is her primary concern whenever they take to the field.

'My biggest thing, and it's always been my biggest thing, is that they come through safely. I would be the same whether they're playing football or camogie, rugby or Australian football. Just so long as they don't get hurt, that's always the big thing for me.

'I know the result is important for them but it isn't as important for me. The most important thing is that she's safe after it.'

Ailish was no stranger to the AFLW when she first signed up for the inaugural Premiership champions. She had previously played for West Clare Waves and the Irish Banshees [the women's national team].

Kay doesn't quite understand all the playing rules, but she's developed a certain sense of familiarity by extension of Ailish's involvement in the sport over the years.

Following an almost flawless campaign, the Adelaide Crows are back in the Grand Final and Ailish has played a major role in helping them book their place in the decider. She kicked two goals in the last three weeks of the season, having been dropped for their Round 6 clash with the Greater Western Sydney (GWS) Giants.

Given the prolific form Considine is showing in front of goal lately, she's almost certain to make an appearance in the decider at some stage after making the match-day squad.

Adelaide secured their spot in the Grand Final after defeating the Geelong Cats in the Preliminary Final last weekend. The quick turnaround didn't give Kay long to arrange the flights, but she will be watching on in the Adelaide Oval on Sunday.

Starting in Shannon Airport, Kay and her son Keith travelled to Heathrow and Dubai before touching down in sunny Adelaide just before the weekend.

Ailish didn't know it, but Eimear tagged along with them and gave her sister quite the shock when she arrived for a surprise visit at the airport.

'I'm overwhelmed and excited,' says Kay.

'It's been such a whirlwind, it's actually kind of crazy. When I finished work yesterday evening, I had to head down to Limerick to pick up a few presents that Ailish wanted me to get, but oh my God, I haven't had a minute.

'It's absolutely amazing. It's been absolutely crazy. It's brilliant, all the good wishes and everything. It's amazing.'

There's certainly been a groundswell of local support for Ailish in the build-up to the game, and another Kilmhil native was hoping he could go to the Grand Final.

Mike Currane of AFLW Ireland grew up just a few miles away from the Considine household and has known Ailish from a young age.

He knew her as a West Clare Waves player and was her head coach when she first joined the Banshees.

Her potential to thrive as an AFLW player was obvious to him from the outset.

'I remember Ailish just came onto the pitch and I handed her a Sherrin and said, 'Kick it.' And that was it, the rest is history.

'She scored 17 goals on that first blitz day in Dublin and won three or four competitions with West Clare Waves. She went on to play for the Irish Banshees, I was lucky to be her head coach on that team as well.'

Currane was instrumental in Considine landing an AFLW contract.

When the aforementioned international camp took place in Melbourne last year, Currane travelled with her and the other Irish players who were selected to take part. The camp was co-ordinated by the CrossCoders programme, and Currane was their Irish point of contact.

As it turned out, Donegal's Yvonne Bonner was selected by GWS Giants, Tipperary forward Aisling McCarthy linked up with the Western Bulldogs, and Collingwood signed Mayo star Sarah Rowe.

Currane suspected that Considine had a strong chance of

being picked up by a club on account of her playing experience.

And when the Crows presented her with a deal, he was there to see Considine put pen to paper.

Currane has been with her almost every step of the way so far, but he can't be there for the Grand Final.

'I literally spent the last three days [trying to get there] and I've had to make a call that I'm not going to be able to make it.

'As much as I'd love to, I'm not going to be over there. I'll watch it live here in the office for sure.

'It's expensive and a long journey but that wasn't even a factor, I'd have gone at the drop of a hat. I just wasn't able to sort stuff with work and that. I'm absolutely delighted that her mam and brother are going and her family will be there to share the occasion with her.

'I'll be dropping her a message and keeping in touch with her.'

Currane has watched all of the Crows' games this season, keeping a particular eye on Considine's performances.

He's been in regular contact with her throughout and while he could tell that her confidence took a knock after being dropped, he wasn't surprised to see her roar back into contention in the next round.

'She's been very consistent all the way through from their practice matches. She's doing everything right. She probably had her poorest performance in Round 5 against the Kangaroos and was dropped for the following round.

'She was devastated at that so it was great to see her back in Round 7 against the Melbourne Demons and she got those two goals in literally two minutes.

'That's a huge monkey off her back as well. I know how

much she's a natural forward and she was probably playing a bit deeper in some of the other games so it was fantastic she got her name on the scoreboard.'

Of course, there was some uncertainty around her availability for the final while she was being assessed, but Currane always felt confident that she would get the green light.

Kay knows that her daughter doesn't engage in rough play when she's on the field, but she jokingly remarks that Ailish was more physical than normal in the Preliminary Final.

'I don't know where I got her because I'm a stresser, she never stresses. She was saying not to book the flights because of the review for the tackle, and she says, 'But don't stress.'

'It wasn't a deliberate tackle. Even in football, Ailish wouldn't be known [for rough play], I think she got one yellow card in her life. She wouldn't be known as a dirty player anyway.

'She was a bit vigorous in her tackle now the last day, I saw an aggression in her I hadn't seen before.'

The Adelaide Crows have lost just one game this season on the way to the Grand Final. That one-point defeat to the Western Bulldogs came back in the opening round, and since then, the Crows have come through most of their games by comfortable winning margins.

Even their Preliminary Final opponents Geelong Cats were 66 points adrift of them at the end of the clash.

Currane is confident that they can reclaim the Premiership title they won two years ago, but in the same breath, he warns that 'nothing is guaranteed' in a Grand Final.

The Crows defeated the other finalists Carlton earlier this year, and repeating that feat in the decider will be a huge challenge for the Adelaide side.

Up to now, Kay has been mainly watching replay footage of Ailish's games. The time difference 'is a bit of a bugger', meaning she couldn't catch the live coverage of the ties.

Luckily, she won't have that problem this Sunday as she prepares to take her seat among the crowd to hopefully watch her daughter get some game time.

She made a promise at the start of this journey and she intends to keep it.

'It's amazing, it's like a fairytale and unbelievable really,' Kay says.

'Ailish has said this umpteen times that there's no words for it and there are no words for how we're feeling about it all.'

FIVE

THE CHAMPION GOLFER

—

RYAN BAILEY

HUGHIES. 421 YARDS. Par 4.

Benign in appearance, yet devilishly tight off the tee. With internal out-of-bounds stakes flanking the fairway on either side, anything pushed or nervously tugged is punished. Just keep it in play.

All week, spectators have filtered in and out of the three grandstands enclosing the opening tee at Royal Portrush. Watch for half an hour, and then move on. The weather has dictated as much. But not on Sunday afternoon at the Open Championship, and not when Shane Lowry is leading by four shots. Standing on the cusp of sporting history. Of Irish sporting immortality.

The wind, as it has done for most of the week, is gusting. But today it's up to 35mph by the time Lowry makes the final walk from the range, via the player's bridge, towards the first tee. 1.47pm, Sunday 21 July. Make a good swing. Just keep it in play.

The dastardly white stakes appear above the billowing rough in the distance. Just in the eyeline as David Lancaster —

the first-tee announcer — invites the colourful and boisterous home crowd to serenade the leader for the first, and certainly not the last, time that afternoon. Don't miss right, don't miss left. Just keep it in play.

To have an internal out-of-bounds marker on a hole is rare on any golf course, but to have two on the same hole is unique. The tented village down the right demands white stakes on that side, but the ruling on the left — where Rory McIlroy found trouble — dates back years. It all comes from when Royal Portrush didn't own a small triangle of land between the 18th and first hole, and the club's members still play the course that way.

'On the tee from the Republic of Ireland, Shane Lowry.'

A guttural roar, in a part of the island where mythical giants have strode the rugged terrain, that could be heard as far away as Clara, 190 miles down the road. Goosebumps. Nerves. Anticipation. History. Make a good swing. Just keep it in play.

Lowry has gone par-birdie-par on Hughies in his run to the top of the leaderboard. It is, in many ways, an eminently agreeable first hole when you're leading a Major, but Lowry had been here before. Not at Portrush, but Oakmont, and even the number of shots he led by — four — could be immediately traced back to that day three years previous. Scars remained, and doubts must have permeated the thought process.

'A little part of me was thinking, not this situation again,' Alan Lowry, Shane's younger brother, admits. 'We had been in that situation before. Not the same circumstances but he had hit that first tee-shot leading a Major before and it didn't go well.'

An hour-and-a-half earlier, Lowry made the short journey from the house he was staying in for the week to the course, alongside his wife Wendy, daughter Iris, manager Brian Moran, close friend Alan Clancy and Alan. The key has always been to have a small, tight-knit entourage. Nothing was going to, or needed to, change now.

Lowry cut a relaxed figure on the practice ground, his external demeanour completely at odds with what he was feeling inside. On the range, he goes through the bag, his coach Neil Manchip dropping balls by his feet, offering gentle pointers.

The previous 16 hours in the house had been a time-passing exercise, an impossible challenge in distracting yourself from over-thinking every shot ahead. But the most important, for so many reasons, was Lowry's first on Sunday afternoon. He must have played it over in his head thousands of times that morning. Just keep it in play.

'Having played the game myself, you know how quickly things can unravel,' Alan continues. 'All of us went to bed that Saturday night wondering was this it, was Shane going to win the Open? It's impossible not to get ahead of yourself, but then you remember what's to come and how quickly it can all change.'

Tommy Fleetwood arrows one down the middle, as easy as you like. Tricolours everywhere, Lowry steps up. Just keep it in play.

'I just can't imagine how it was hitting that first tee-shot,' Alan says. 'I was in the stand and all I was thinking was 'just hit it between the out-of-bounds posts'. Honestly, that's all I was thinking. I could barely watch. I can't imagine how tough it was for him.'

Once the noise died down, Lowry stood over it with three-wood in hand. Danger right, calamity left. Palms sweaty, hearts in mouths. And left it went, Lowry's swing not as fluid and true as he would have liked, the marshals nervously signalling towards those damn white stakes. The entire crowd — the entire nation — held their collective breath as the ball bounded in the direction of destruction. Who knows what would have happened had it ended up on the wrong side of those stakes. But it didn't, coming down just short in the thick rough. In play. Relief.

Lowry hit 72 shots during the final round and 269 strokes over the course of the four days, but none were more important than those first couple of swings on Sunday afternoon. To ease the nerves, to settle into it. Not only because of what had happened in Oakmont, but because a field of lavish quality was waiting to pounce on any slip-up, any sign of weakness.

'I was standing with Neil in the crowd at the back of the first green and we couldn't see a thing,' Alan, an accomplished golfer himself having won the prestigious Mullingar Scratch Cup, recalls.

'It was about 10 deep around the green and we were literally just waiting for a groan or a roar. It was a sickening wait because we knew that first hole was crucial, just the way it played out.'

With Fleetwood missing his birdie attempt, Lowry then held his nerve to drain a clutch putt for bogey to ensure there wasn't an early two-shot swing on the first green. Pars on two and three followed and he was able to settle into the round, into the occasion.

'Having watched Shane for the last decade, and even being on the bag for him a few times, there are always little signs I look out for when he's playing. Just small things that show he's happy or confident. On the fourth tee, he took out the three wood again and just ripped it down the middle. It was a really solid swing, and from there, I just knew he was on it.'

Lowry followed a booming three wood with a gorgeous four iron into six feet on the fourth. A silky smooth putt disappeared into the cup and his lead had been extended to five, before he showed off his short-game wizardry to card two further birdies before the turn. Oh, he was on it alright. In complete control of his own game, enchanting the rain-soaked galleries with golf for the ages.

Just as he had done during Saturday's superlative, blemish-free round of 63, Lowry conjured a dominant display from tee to green to leave his pursuers trailing in his wake and turn his Carnoustie tears into glorious triumph in the space of 12 transformative months.

'I don't get overly emotional watching Shane,' Alan continues. 'But when he birdied 15, I don't even know who I was with, to be honest, but I just remember thinking, my big brother is going to win the Open.

'I was then walking up towards the 18th when he was on the 17th tee and I got a photo in a Whatsapp group of them carving Shane's name onto the Claret Jug and that's when it really hit me. It just hit me. He's the Open champion. It was very surreal, it's still surreal.'

On a difficult, wintery day of intermittent rain and gusting gales, there was only one man on the links commanding the conditions. Lowry controlled the golf course, the golf ball, his temperament, the occasion and his destiny to become the fifth Irishman to lift that famous piece of sporting silverware.

With the crowds packed so deep on virtually every tee-box, fairway and green, it was almost impossible for everyone to actually witness Lowry at his masterful best as he surged towards a truly remarkable six-shot victory. But, whatever the vantage point, thousands will claim to have been there the day Shane Lowry was crowned Open champion.

The scenes as the Clara native made his way up the 18th, arms aloft and a smile as wide as the fairway, were truly special and emotional, memories to last a lifetime for everyone inside and outside the rope. Just as they were in Abu Dhabi last January when Lowry ended his three-and-a-half-year barren run, Wendy and Iris were first on the green to greet their champion.

'I was actually fine emotionally all day and then I went in behind and met Shane's manager Brian and I gave him a hug and I lost it,' Alan says.

'I just started crying and I couldn't stop. It was just so overwhelming and even then when we saw him coming up to the green… all the family were just bawling their eyes out. It was the most surreal moment I've ever experienced. It's just so hard to explain.'

What made this win all the more remarkable was that it was forged from the depths of despair. A year previous, having missed the Open cut — his fourth successive at the championship — Lowry admitted he wasn't in love with golf and golf wasn't in love with him. His form had gone stale, that burgeoning potential had threatened to expire before he had truly reached his peak.

'A lot of the emotion for me came from having seen him get through the tough times,' Alan continues. 'It was just so unbelievable to see. I don't think he felt he was getting what he wanted out of the game and then all of a sudden it just turned around.'

Just like it would be too simplistic to say the player-caddie relationship formed with Bo Martin has sparked Lowry's revival in 2019, it is also presumptuous to say his new-found perspective in fatherhood and married life has helped him play better golf. But what is certain is that Lowry is in a much better headspace.

While most players feel they need to be obsessive to become a Major winner, it was refreshing to witness Lowry join an illustrious club when, as he said himself, golf matters less to him now than it did a few years ago when he surrendered a four-shot lead at the US Open.

That he won his maiden Major on the island of Ireland, to a unique background of choruses of *Óle, Óle, Óle* and *Shano, Shano, Shano* on the County Antrim links, made it all the more memorable. It is hard to think of a more popular winner.

'We have more than 20 aunts and uncles and nearly all of them were there that afternoon,' Alan explains. 'Sure even in the player's lounge after, I was there trying to convince the woman who runs it that these were actually all our family. There were a good 50 people. It was mental.

'Having a big family, we don't all see each other too often, but to come together on an occasion like that was brilliant. I remember even walking over the bridge from the 18th down towards the media, a few of our aunts and uncles were there waiting and we just went insane. I'm even getting emotional thinking about it now. It was amazing. We'll never forget it.'

And of all the iconic images — from the first tee, to the dam bursting and the crowds converging on the 18th — that will forever be immortalised, one stands out above all else. Mum and Dad, Bridget and Brendan, brother Alan and sister Sinéad. Shane. And the Claret Jug. One for the living room.

'That's hands down my favourite photo of all time,' Alan beams. 'The second I saw it, I just knew it was the best photo I'll ever have.

'In terms of wins in the future, I don't think anything can top this. I hope he gets close and does stuff like this again, but I don't know if this can be topped.'

In the land of myths and legends, Shane Lowry — 10 years on from his breakthrough moment in Baltray — fulfilled his true destiny on the Royal Portrush links. The 2019 Open winner. The champion golfer.

SIX

AN OFFICER AND A GAA MANAGER

—

KEVIN O'BRIEN | 28 AUGUST

IN HIS MIND'S eye, Jim Gavin can still picture the scene like it was yesterday.

The year is 1990 and it's a wet, miserable morning at the Curragh Camp in Kildare.

An 18-year-old Gavin has just been dropped off by his parents to join the 67th Cadet Class of the Defence Forces.

He's wearing one of his father Jimmy's old suits that's a couple of sizes too big for him, sporting 'big floppy hair' and holding a retro briefcase-style suitcase in one hand as he waves goodbye to his parents with the other.

It's a seminal moment in the young life of the Clondalkin native. Much of what he has achieved in the GAA, the six senior All-Ireland titles — one as a player and five as a manager — can be traced back to the man that was formed and shaped through his military career.

Only weeks earlier, Gavin had started his third-level studies when a letter arrived in the post saying he was accepted into the Defence Forces. His dream was to become a pilot and to do so he was required to enlist as an Air Corps cadet.

The Defence Forces took on just 30 cadets each year with only six of them qualifying for the Air Corps.

'I was delighted to get the opportunity,' he recalls. 'The Defence Forces looked after me really well. I couldn't speak highly enough of the career I had, and the great time I had.

'I've great, fond memories of my experiences there. Travelled the world. I've some great friends from the military.'

He was brought to the limits both mentally and physically during those early days in the Curragh and throughout his subsequent aviation career with the United Nations that took him to what he calls 'the dark heart of Africa'.

But the toughest part of the journey for Gavin came at the very outset, a moment that's ingrained in his mind.

'Waving goodbye to my mum and dad who had just handed their son over to the Defence Forces, that was probably the hardest thing,' he says.

'They had obviously looked after me so well growing up. Everything else was a massive challenge. Cadet training is very, very demanding. A lot of my class left and said, 'Not for me'.

'But that's probably the hardest thing. Once you get into it, like everything else, we'd great fun, great comrades, great friends that training makes for life.'

That floppy head of hair didn't last long after his arrival.

'I remember it well. I was marched over to Pearse Hall — all the buildings there are named after the leaders of 1916. I'd say it was gone inside of the hour.

'I sat on the seat, with Reggie Darling, people in the Curragh camp will know who Reggie Darling is. His one job was to shave that floppy hair off my head and make it bald.

'I'm not going to say the shouting, but the orders began at that moment to Cadet Gavin.

'Great memories. I'm shaking now,' he admits.

A few years ago, the Defence Forces released some video footage of the training that Gavin's Cadet class underwent between '90 and '92.

The military training was deliberately tough so nothing they encountered while deployed would be as intimidating as those tests in camp.

'They mould you, absolutely,' Gavin says.

'You're essentially raw when you go in there. Our generation were all very fortunate to have opportunities that our parents might not have had, and our grandparents certainly never had.

'So we probably grew up in a very sterile environment. The Defence Forces certainly prepare you for... Well, they're an armed force.

'Their role ultimately, like an insurance policy, is to protect the citizens of the state from ultimate aggression. The very end of it — their job is to put their life on the line or to possibly take the life of somebody else, at the very worst case.

'That takes a lot of discipline, a lot of training to mould somebody into that mindset. To have the discipline to have that and use it in the appropriate manner, is something that probably doesn't get acknowledged enough about our Defence Forces personnel who are there as our backstop.

'So yeah, it was a great experience and that service of something higher than yourself, as in serving your state. I wore the uniform of the state, with Óglaigh na hÉireann (Defence Forces) for 20 years and I was very proud to do so.

'Each day you'd get up and stand to attention as the national flag was raised. At the end of the day, at sunset, you'd stand to attention as the national flag was brought back down. That's in my blood, that sense of service from a very young age.

'I graduated from the cadet school as a second lieutenant, essentially as an infantry officer, platoon commander. So you're taught all those leadership skills at a very young age, which I've been trading off in my life ever since.'

Gavin played minor football with Dublin in 1988 and '89 before his army career took precedence. He wasn't part of the U21 side that reached the Leinster final in 1992, but the following year made his senior debut under manager Dr Pat O'Neill.

By 1995, he was an All-Ireland winner at 24 years old. That season Gavin fulfilled the role of what we now know as a modern wing-forward. O'Neill recognised that Gavin had the attributes required for the position.

He wasn't the most talented player on the squad but he was hard-working, intelligent and versatile. He was tasked with nullifying the influence of attacking half-backs against both Meath and Cork.

'He was strong, small, good fitness, good footballing technique with his left foot,' says Charlie Redmond, who was full-forward on that side.

'When he came into the team in 1995, he was brought in to do a marking job on Graham Geraghty. He did such a good job, he was kept on to mark Ciarán O'Sullivan — he did a good job there too. He was well able to do a job.

'Not only was he able to do a job though, he was well able to play football as well. He was a lovely man to boot. He always had a love for the game, he always had a love for the behind-the-scenes stuff too. We also know that he's a pilot by trade so he's by the book, he knows the importance of sticking religiously to what you know is good and what works.'

Like a good army man, Gavin was given a brief and he carried it out to the letter. Small in stature, he was a fiery competitor that was prepared to do what it took to win.

'If you gave Jim a job to do, he would get that job done,' adds Redmond.

'He would stick zealously to it, and then he might broaden the parameters of that job. Just like an army man would, you tell him to do something, he'll do it. If it wasn't done, it wasn't for the want of effort.'

Given his defensive wing-forward role, the army lads would poke fun at Gavin for years after '95, calling him the best wing-back Dublin ever had.

The latter part of Gavin's Dublin career overlapped with the first six years or so of Johnny Magee's. He could spot the influence of Gavin's military training on his football a mile off.

'He was very meticulous with how he went about his training and stuff,' says the Kilmacud manager.

'You can see those attributes in the lads today. On the field, Jim always gave everything. There was no quarter given with him. He gave 110%, it was always the way he went about his training and how he played his football.

'As a guy away from the field I couldn't speak highly enough of the guy. He always gave time to me. He's just a generally good guy.'

Gavin's Dublin career ended in 2002 and Tommy Lyons suggested he and Declan Darcy fill the void by training a talented Dublin U21 side that was emerging. The team that featured future stars Alan Brogan and Bryan Cullen delivered Dublin's first All-Ireland at the grade in 2003.

Magee says Gavin was destined to move into coaching after he called time on his inter-county career.

'Himself and Deccie [Darcy] were the coaches. You could see the lads were eager to get in there and they had the grá for it.

'I think they were at that stage of their career where they knew they were coming to the end of their careers. I think they were looking forward to fill that void that was going to happen after you finish playing football.'

He drifted away from management for a few years as his work took hold once again.

He returned to lead the U21s to All-Ireland glory in 2010 and 2012 before assuming his current role with the senior team ahead of the 2013 campaign.

By that stage, Gavin had risen through the ranks of the Air Corps, operated as its chief flying instructor and flown the government jet before his move to the Irish Aviation Authority.

'Obviously the aviation industry and aviation itself teaches you so much about managing teams, as in your flight crew as opposed to a football team,' he says.

'Aviation, by its nature, the reasons we have commercial air transport has become so safe and we take it as second nature to go fly an aircraft, a medium-bodied aircraft, max take-off weight would be about 80 tonnes, full of fuel, two big engines, 150 degree celsius on fuel, it's the norm now.

'But the reasons we have assumed it's so safe is it's an industry that learns from its lessons. So I've always taken that. There's great lessons to be learned from our game against Mayo. It's a rich environment for learning, for each challenge that you face.

'We'll try and take as much as we can from that game in preparation for the next game.'

While the perception may be that life in the military is extremely regimented, Gavin's experience suggested otherwise and it has shaped his management philosophy.

'It's probably one perception of armed forces. But from a leadership perspective, because I was taught that as an officer, you're taught those leadership skills, you gain control by giving control away.

'Which is another way of saying you empower people. Ultimately as a platoon commander on the battlefield, you can't control every section of the platoon, every rifle of the platoon. They need to make a choice on the field of play. So they're the skills.

'Even though it comes across as a very authoritarian style, if you're in a battle, I was fortunate to serve overseas with the United Nations in an Irish uniform, you're in some very hostile environments.

'So there has to be a very direct command and a very precise control, because obviously you have weapons and you're putting people's lives on the line. Thankfully that's not the case in sport. But the principles still remain the same.

'You empower people. You're serving them and the officer and the troops. Myself and the management team are serving the players. We're enabling them to be their very best, that's all you're trying to do. Being your best has many, many guises.

'We embrace diversity, we want guys to be different, to think differently. We like having guys from different backgrounds, who have different tastes in music, different tastes in whatever.

'We see that as a strength rather than a perception that everyone needs to be robots. That's the last thing we want.'

In many ways it was his experience serving overseas with the UN that defined the Dublin manager. His time there brought him all over the world into some exceedingly hostile environments. It was a life-changing experience.

'I served with the United Nations, a 12,000-troop contingent in Chad,' he explains. 'My role was in force headquarters and chief of the military aviation was my title.

'Controlling air assets, from MI26 helicopters, MI28s to various other transport aircrafts from Bangladesh, Canada, Norway. But that particular country is called the dark heart of Africa for a very good reason.

'On its west is Cameroon, the north is Libya, to the south is the Central African Republic, CAR. But to its east is a country called Sudan, and there's a conflict called Darfur which was the land of Fur which kind of goes into the eastern part of Chad.

'In the countryside, for every five kids who are born, three are dead by the age of five. Horrific conditions. I spent a lot of time on the ground as well with Nepalese and Mongolian troops, walking the land.

'So that certainly gave you a perspective on life, and makes you very humble and grateful for what you have on this little island on the northwest corner of Europe, that's closer to the poles than we are to the Equator.

'But we have a relatively stable democracy, good economy generally speaking, and lots of opportunities for you to excel. So it makes you very grateful for what you have.'

So when it comes to talk about the five-in-a-row and what's at stake on Sunday, Gavin can retain a good deal of perspective.

'That's it. There's obviously a lot at stake for both counties, a lot of expectations. But, yeah I've been fortunate.

'And in the aviation industry as well, as one who is exposed as someone who regulates the industry, and one who sees on a regular basis incidents and accidents and fatalities, and understands how fragile life can be.

'I've lost some great friends, some very close friends, pilots in aviation accidents. Life can be very fickle. So it probably informs my view on the sporting world that there are no guarantees.

'You just turn up every day, and all we have done by winning an All-Ireland semi-final is to earn the right to perform in another game, and that's simply it. If you can perform to the best of your ability, hopefully you'll be there or thereabouts at the end of the game.'

SEVEN

COFFEE AT THE CROSSROADS

—

SEAN FARRELL | 24 MARCH

THE COFFEE SHOP hums away unabated, steam jets out into cups, music plays in the background and the bottom falls from the stage Michael Allen has been making a living on.

'Mike, there's no easy way to say this. The contract's no longer there.'

Having made his professional rugby debut in 2011, Allen moved from Ulster to Edinburgh in 2015 seeking a change of scenery and a settled position.

A versatile back boasting electric pace, which took him out of the centre to the wing more often than he would have liked, there was a sense that Allen could even benefit from a three-year residency rule and see international rugby for Scotland before this year's World Cup.

Whatever the prospects, he felt utterly welcomed and at home in his new club and his new home city and, as he turned 26, was more than happy to re-sign when contract discussions came up in 2016.

In the lead-up to that Christmas, he was under the impression that the deal was agreed and simply awaiting a signature. But Hogmanay came and went, January and February too. Still no word. It fell to Duncan Hodge, Edinburgh's interim head coach, to bear the bad news that somebody's opinion of Allen's future had shifted.

'The whole time I had been thinking things will be fine, happy days. To be hit with that bombshell was pretty horrendous,' Allen says. 'I remember saying to Duncan Hodge that Wednesday morning, 'I've a wife and a baby on the way.

'She's due in July.'

* * *

When *The42* first got in contact with Allen last month, he was basking in bright Alpine sunshine, wrapped up against the cold of a ski-slope and thoroughly enjoying the sort of time off that seemed so alien to him as a professional rugby player.

The turmoil of losing a job and switching away from a career many view as a dream has all been smoothed out.

It worked out for the best and he holds no regrets, but if he wishes anything had turned out differently, it's the timeline. A little extra warning that a move was necessary to further his rugby career would have given him a level playing field. But three months out from the end of the campaign, most clubs have their business done.

'I remember sitting in the hotel saying to the wife, 'What am I going to do? I don't know how I'm going to make money.''

Before that, his flight of fancy had always been to take up a scissors and shears. There was a barbering qualification tucked away in the drawer and the broad strokes of his plan had been to open his own shop and snip away from his mid-30s on. But that wasn't a serious option any more. Not with a child on the way and no nest egg to kick-start a new business.

The choices were clear: he could chase the dream as a rugby player, up sticks, switch clubs and push for five more years in his current career, or he could get started on the next one.

'And those five years could be a year at one club, a year at another,' adds Allen. 'You could be hopping around. I don't have anything against guys who do that, I just wasn't up for it and that's just me.'

His wife Eireann was prepared to hit the road and bring a newborn along. After all, what Pro D2 lacks in on-field glamour, it makes up for with the backdrop of places like Biarritz, Beziers and Carcassonne. However, the prospect of clocking up clubs and kit did not appeal to Allen half as much as continuing to build his life in Edinburgh and doing so around his wife and daughter — rather than the other way around.

That sounded like value and a quality use of his time.

'I didn't want to drop down a level just to pick up a pay cheque, even if the pay cheque was substantial… it probably seemed a strange decision, but looking back now, I'm happy where I am.'

When the time came to say goodbye to the game in a tux at Edinburgh's end of season awards, he had already sat an exam and had himself bound for a day job which demanded a suit rather than boots.

Allen was put into contact with Chris Tweed and set about working and studying his way through a different sort of academy system, towards a role in financial services.

'I owe a massive amount to Tweed Wealth Management for taking me on,' says Allen.

'It was a pretty rough time: you've got a baby on the way in three or four months' time, no new contract — what are you going to do?'

Throughout it all, Eireann remained a constant for Allen. Though she was content to move elsewhere if needed, as a doctor studying to qualify as an anaesthetist, the lure of a job in the Royal Hospital was a strong tether to keep roots in the Scottish capital.

'She's very happy, she's very good at her job and is well-respected and regarded.

'She actually did her last exam when she was 36-weeks pregnant. She went down to London for that which was, eh… a bit of a laugh.'

Not all heroes wear capes.

* * *

'I remember standing there thinking: 'This is Ronan O'Gara!"

Allen doesn't have a pre-formed list of go-to highlights to turn to when we ask about his fondest memories of rugby. He genuinely racks his brain and the moments that jump out are not individual flourishes where he is skating around defenders to ground a try. They are collective efforts with just a fleck of a sense of new beginning and fresh starts about them on a personal level.

When he mentions O'Gara, it's in the context of a 'made-it' moment early in the 2012/13 season. Allen was manning the left wing, maintaining the line's integrity with All Black great

Doug Howlett directly opposite him, and O'Gara, the expert at pulling matches from the fire, working in tandem with Conor Murray to probe this way and that in search of a gap and any weakness in Ulster.

Munster cranked through 23 phases' worth of pressure, but could not turn the 20-19 deficit around. Securing that win gave Allen a sense of momentum in his chosen field as he nods to a win over Glasgow two weeks earlier — though he doesn't breathe a word of the match-turning try he scored.

A more meaningful win over Glasgow is the second fond memory that springs to mind. The back-to-back successes for Edinburgh in the '1872' derby clashes gave him his only medal as a professional, and helped him feel fully embedded in his new club after an ill-timed run of injuries during his first six months by the North Sea.

He donned an Ireland jersey in 2013 and 2014 as part of Emerging Ireland squads sent to Georgia and Romania, where he played with the likes of Rhys Ruddock, Jordi Murphy, Tiernan O'Halloran, Tommy O'Donnell and Ian Keatley.

He believes he was capable of achieving more in his career, yet he's at peace with that.

'I'm proud of what I did achieve. I'm completely okay with the fact that I think I under-achieved. I always wanted to play international, always wanted to get 50, 100 caps for Ulster. That's not the case and I'm completely fine with that now.

'I wasn't when I was playing. I just have a very different outlook on career, lifestyle and things like that. I'm a much more relaxed person now than I was when I was playing.

'It was disappointing because I did aspire to be an international, but when it came down to it, I wasn't good enough.

I was a decent player, I played quite a lot, but I wasn't good enough to play internationally. I know that now.

'When I was playing, you have to have aspirations and goals, but now that I've left rugby, I don't have any problem being truthful about it.'

Indeed, those moments when he fell short in his past career may have been a blessing in disguise as he can now reap the benefits in 'the afterlife'.

'Maybe it was the type of player I was. I wasn't an international, wasn't a household name. I finished and went, 'Right, that was good, what next?'

'Some guys who are more high profile find it more difficult to move away, but I knew I couldn't make money out of rugby any more when I retired. I wasn't that type of guy.

'Stevie Ferris has got his punditry and all, but he's a Lion, he's one of the best back rows to ever play for Ulster. He can do that with his name, but there are a lot of players who think they can go on with rugby because of their name, but it's not big enough.

'I wasn't a superstar so it didn't hit me like a ton of bricks. I could go play golf, go skiing, and spend time with my family and my kid.

'People say, 'Do you miss it?' And I say not at all and that's the truth. I don't miss it at all.'

The longer Allen speaks, the better the quiet life sounds. At work, his boss is a fellow Ulsterman and he works alongside another Irish former rugby player in Paul Rowley.

The office provides enough of that dressing room-style back-and-forth to fulfil the camaraderie many sportspeople miss when they hang up their boots. And the rest is quality family time.

He has made the transition in incredibly smooth fashion and he knows how grateful he ought to be for that, cognisant of the many who struggled mentally with the same change of circumstances.

Allen is not settling with life outside of sport. He is thriving in it.

The freedom he feels is palpable. It's about more than just heading for the slopes to ski, a pursuit all too risky when earning a living with your body. It's every single weekend, every evening, and every last meal choice.

'Now I don't mind sharing a bottle of wine of a Tuesday night. With rugby, it's never something you can do,' he says with a laugh.

'Just having the ability to have a weekend. I can fly back to Belfast, don't have to ask. Just book it and go.

'What you sacrifice as a rugby player is so much more than anyone gives any player credit for. The weddings you miss, best friends' birthdays or even, my wife's a very good snowboarder and the jealousy of seeing her go away on a ski trip for a week was just so annoying.

'You do sacrifice a hell of a lot. To be able to come out of it and be happy and to have a good job with a longevity and be able to have a nice life with my family in Edinburgh is quite nice.

'I don't feel guilty about not eating well — I never had a couple of takeaways in a week, but if I had I'd be dwelling on it — 'That's really bad' — whereas now, pfft! Fine. I'll get to the gym once in about three months.'

The absence of a fitness regime is one aspect Allen does miss, but he is content to wait a while longer before pushing tin again in the future.

He has taken the odd bike ride and the odd run on top of those quarterly gym visits. Add a tendency to sustain himself with breakfast and coffee during busy days when he's kept on the go and it all amounts to the loss of muscle mass.

He has a rack of old suits which now look like they belong to another man.

'Since January it's been New Year, same me,' he jokes, 'but it's either go to the gym after work or do bath and bed with the baby.

'She'd go down at seven most nights and by the time that's done all I want to do is sit and watch a show with my wife.

'I'm never going to be the size I was and that's just what it is. I've suits up there in my wardrobe and they just hang off me. I'm not going to try and work my way into filling them.'

* * *

Looking back on the pivotal coffee shop meeting that swept one career path away and brought him to the current state of contentment, Allen has held on to no ill will.

Hodge was clearly left in a difficult position as interim head coach and Allen feels the backs specialist did him a good turn by finally getting the bad news confirmed.

Current Edinburgh head coach Richard Cockerill was announced as the new incoming boss in the weeks before Allen's fate was sealed, but if the 26-year-old was bitter, the 28-year-old has cleansed his palate.

'Maybe a new coach comes in and he could think, 'He's not what I want going forward', and that's fine. I don't really hold a grudge. I did for a while, because it was very sudden.

'If I could change how they dealt with me, rather than stringing me along for those months, I could have gotten my head around it. But they told me in March and then you only have two months to find a club if you do want to keep playing rugby and that's just too short a time.'

Allen liberally drops in phrases like 'I wasn't good enough' when he's chatting about international honours, be they at U20 or Test level, but he was unquestionably cut out for high-level professional rugby and surely would not have had to spend long out of the top divisions had he chosen that route.

Instead he took an incredibly mature, long-term option over the obvious 'dream'. He chose the best thing for him and his family.

'I gave up rugby because I wanted to. I wasn't forced to stop. I could have kept playing, but I was happy to say I'm going to go into something completely new and different. Start studying again for the first time in eight years.'

It wasn't a completely clean break from rugby. Allen bridged out of 'the bubble' by playing with Watsonians last season, but since the summer, rugby holds a role of diminishing importance in his life.

He checks the scores to see how his former clubs got on, but he doesn't have to build his weekends around the fixture schedule. And so he doesn't.

EIGHT

WALK OF LIFE

—

PAUL FENNESSY | 24 MARCH

AT 25, IT already feels as if Kate Veale's life could be a movie script, albeit one still awaiting the classic Hollywood ending.

The Waterford native was an immensely gifted athlete who at one stage appeared to have a genuine chance of winning an Olympic medal. And then, all of a sudden, she disappeared, going completely off the radar. So what happened?

To understand her story, it is necessary to go back to her life growing up. An only child, her parents were a big influence. Both were involved in athletics to an extent, particularly her father, who ran regularly, competing in marathons, with a personal best in the 2:40s.

'He always had this passion,' Veale explains. 'He never got to international or whatever. It was just out running every day for the enjoyment.

'He'd be getting up at 8am on a Sunday morning to go off and do 25-mile runs, it was just normal. Just going to races and all that, it was always around me I suppose. It's gas having that in the house, it's not like it was pushed on you, it was just what you wanted to do. You just follow on.'

It soon became apparent that like her father, Veale had a passion for running. She took up cross country in her school, St Augustine's College, and quickly excelled.

'My first major race was a cross-country race in Paris in 2005 that I won,' she recalls. 'It was then that I said 'I really want to have a proper go at this and get to an Olympics."

However, fate would take Veale in a different direction ultimately.

'It was the East Munsters or something. Someone said: 'Can you just step in there for the walk for points with the school?' My main event really was the 1500m on the track. I stepped in for the walk. I got a bit of flair for the technique. I started training. So I was doing both [racewalking and cross country]. At U18, I won the national cross country and I went to the European Junior Cross Country in 2011.

'At the time, I was trying to do both and then I made a decision to go with walking — I had more opportunities and stuff, so I decided then to make a proper go of it.'

Around the time of the 2004 Olympics, Veale was left feeling inspired after Irish racewalking star Rob Heffernan paid a visit to her club. And having crossed paths with an elite athlete, Veale then endeavoured to become one.

'I was a bit of a freak,' she says of her early school days. 'I was starting to get serious with running and I was kind of mature for my age. I had this mindset that I was different from the rest of the people in my class. The likes of my parents and coaches would have seen that I was different. I would have done extra training and I would have been very particular about everything.

'Before my time, I was looking up stuff about the science [behind sport]. I suppose some people might have thought I was a bit of a weirdo.'

It was fourth year of secondary school when she felt racewalking started to get really serious. By then, Veale was being coached by Jamie Costin, spending considerable time away from school and even attending a training camp in Spain with the likes of Heffernan and Olive Loughnane.

'Just seeing them, I really wanted to be one of them,' Veale recalls. 'I was trying to be one of them, but it was before my time. I was trying to push my body. Back then, I was naive. I was on an upward slope, I was getting PBs all the time, improving all the time. I was doing everything right, I was in my bubble and this was my life, and this was all I wanted.

'Fourth year, I would have gone to Russia, to European Youths and the Youth Olympics. I was getting all the national records, 15 up to junior, same with all the school records. Every time I went out, I was beating my own records. I was improving all the time. In fifth year, I would have won the World Youths really convincingly. It was funny, I finished that race and I wanted in my age to be the best in the world and I just felt so much confidence, because it was quite easy.

'I would have felt I could have taken on anyone at that stage. But people would have said it and I would have believed it — I'd be like 'I'm going to get an Olympic medal. I'm going to do this. It's just going to improve, it's going to get better, I'm so excited."

Veale also excelled academically. She can't remember her exact results, but the talented athlete received mostly As and got close to 600 points in the Leaving Cert.

'I was a perfectionist and liked people being like: 'Oh, Kate's this and Kate's that' — thinking that I could do it all."

It felt as if Veale's meteoric rise would never abate, but she was about to come cruelly crashing down to earth.

'That year, things started changing. I got a bit of a hip injury. It was the first time I had anything major. I would have had niggles, but it was the first time I started not improving and not being able to do the training and that was frustrating me.

'When I tried to come back, my coach, who was fantastic, was being so careful with me and I wasn't even listening to him. I would say 'I'm after missing training the last few days, so I'm just going to do extra training now.' It was never getting better, it was a vicious cycle. The more training I was doing, the worse I was getting.

'I went to the Youth World Cup, I finished sixth and it was kind of like: 'Aw look, that's just the injury, I'll get over it and I'll come back with World Juniors.'

'I had access to Rob and Olive and everyone, but if things weren't going well, I wouldn't admit it to anyone. I was faking things: 'It's fine, I'll be able to do it.' I wouldn't turn to anyone and was thinking it would always be okay. I did [the World Juniors] race and finished 17th, coming from first the year before, to being lapped and [getting a time] that I would have easily beaten 12 months previously.'

Having started out with physical issues, Veale's problems primarily became psychological thereafter.

'I didn't want to be anything other than an athlete and when I wasn't, I felt so [lacking in identity],' she explains. 'I was known as the athlete in town. Everyone knew of me around the place. I kind of liked that and I wanted to be that. When

I finished 17th, then it was more mentally [I was affected], because I knew I wasn't improving.

'The training got worse, and I kind of just hated the sport then, because I had a bad attitude to it, it was very black and white. If I can't win and I can't be the best, I'm not doing this.

'Mentally, it was just draining, and I suppose I was kind of burnt out. I didn't have anyone pushing me. Someone said to me, 'You are burnt out', and they would have asked about my training or coach or family. It was nothing to do with any of them, it was me.'

Having become disillusioned, Veale stopped competing entirely. She went to Dublin City University to study Sports Science and Health in what was the beginning of a hugely difficult and challenging time in her life. The former starlet could only watch on as many of those she had competed against continued to make waves, competing in the Olympics and other illustrious events.

'I felt like a failure,' she says. 'So many people had invested so much effort and I felt like I'd let them down, thinking: 'I should be that. I could be that."

As she struggled to leave her sporting past behind, Veale's mental health deteriorated.

'That was the hard thing back then — it wasn't me. People were worried about me, my family, my friends, they knew I was different. I was absolutely broken... At the time, you think you're the only one going through it.

'I can't even count how many people and how many different therapies and treatments I've been through. One of them eventually has to click I suppose. I've been through enough.

'People would think: 'Oh, that's it for me.' It was such a rollercoaster. All the time, two steps forward, two steps back. It was so up and down and I was not giving up, even though there'd be days where you're thinking: 'My biology or genetics is just like this now, and I can't do anything about it. This is just me and I won't be able to be happy, I suppose.'

'The funny thing is people don't even know and they'd never think it about me. They were always like: 'How do you do it all? I wouldn't have the [motivation] the way you have.' Back then, people knew me as the athlete and the person that trained all the time. They'd see me out in any type of weather and not out drinking, so I was kind of different. I wanted to be that person: 'I'm tough, I'm strong.' Holding up this ego or something.

'So when the wheels started to come off, it was a big downward spiral. But you don't give into it. I thought: 'I'm mentally strong.' My mind is my greatest advantage and my greatest disadvantage in a sense. I feel I got to the absolute top and I hit rock bottom.

'It got so bad. I was still lying to people, but they knew. There had to be intervention even though I was like: 'No, it's fine.' It actually got to a stage where I gave into it and I was like: 'Yeah, I do need this and I do need help.'

'It was going on for so long and I was hiding it and I was so good at hiding it. I put on this brave face — I'm just doing this and pretending to my coach, and my coach even knew.

'It was funny, I never would cry ever. It was such a difficult moment — I remember being out with my coach training. He knew [something was wrong from] the way I was training. I just stopped training and started crying, and he gave me a hug. I was so embarrassed because: 'I'm tough and I'm able to [deal with adversity].' It was me that drove me to have this burnout. It was: 'I can't be feeling like this. I'm not this person, just get on with it' — that old-school mentality. 'Stop being weak. Stop being such a sissy.'

'It's actually the first time I've said it out properly as well, but if I can help one person [it will be worth it]. My friends at home even, if they see this, they'll be like: 'Really?' Because I would have lied to them. They would have thought I was the strongest of the group or whatever.

'It was so bad that I remember my mam making me go to a counsellor. I went into them and they did an assessment with me. It was: 'Oh, we're sending you straight to hospital.' I was like: 'What? I thought it wasn't that bad.' And that's how bad it got.

'I lied to people at home telling them I was at college. Because it was like: 'No one can know I'm in here.' You're so ashamed.

'After that, I came out of there and it still wasn't right. They wanted to admit me again. It's not a six-week programme and you're better. It's something you have to work on all the time.'

Veale's depression was at its most intense between 2012 and 2014. Having sought professional help, the youngster gradually started to feel better to the extent that she decided to return to training, but fate intervened again.

'I started coming back, doing little bits in the gym and I was out running and stuff. I had only done about 5k and I was getting sick after sessions. 'What the hell?' I was like: 'It must be a fever.' Then I found out I was pregnant.

'I was thinking: 'How can I deal with this? I can't look after myself.'

'I had a baby and people would have thought: 'Oh, sure she won't finish college now and she won't get back into athletics. It was like: 'No.''

Rather than ending her sporting ambitions, the birth of Fianna in 2015 ultimately made Veale more determined to succeed.

'It made me accepting and it made me better myself and it made me strong. I thought: 'I'm actually going to be a better person.'

'It was kind of a moment that made me… People say: 'You have a kid now, it's different.' Yeah, it's different for me, but does it mean I'm not going to the Olympics?

'It's funny because I see that and I want to show [my daughter] what I can do. Having an unplanned pregnancy — sometimes things are just meant to be in your life. You deal with it and you become a better person and your life is better for it.'

Her early attempts at a return in 2016 were tentative.

'I came back, just doing a bit of running for fun. I thought: 'Do you know what? I'm going to do a road race. And if I do it in this time, so what?' I trained with my dad. It was lovely. I did the Dublin Marathon with him. I got that love of sport back.

'I didn't really commit to any proper training. I was just enjoying it and doing bits and pieces. Last year, I came back and was doing a lot of my own stuff. I didn't want coaching, because I felt really bad with someone putting work into me again when I'm not at the top. I felt 'I'm not worthy to be getting a coach. I'm not going to be winning a medal, I'll do my own coaching.''

However, Veale got chatting to Irish Olympian Brendan Boyce, who convinced her to appoint a coach. So well over a decade on from that fateful first meeting in the local club in Waterford, Heffernan agreed to link up with the rejuvenated racewalker.

'I just appreciate what he's doing, because never mind the athletes not getting any money, he's not getting anything and I know there's a coach over in China getting nearly a million a year and there are other coaches on proper salaries. For him to put the effort in and not be getting anything back, it's [admirable]. He has the faith in me and he actually said: 'No, you can do this and your journey is going to be good and you are going to be great again.'

'I've learned so much from him. When we're not training, then we chill. It's about recovery.

'Before I'd be switched on all the time and so particular about everything. But I was freaking out about it and thinking it was a disaster.

'I would have been very black and white before, things had to be perfect. Now it's like: 'There are going to be rough days and awful times.'

'The Olympic qualifications came out last week and I was freaking out and Rob says: 'Calm down, all you can do is get out, do this session and walk today.'

And Veale has made encouraging progress since returning, winning gold at the National 20k Championships last December among other impressive feats.

At the moment, she is balancing life as an athlete with primary school teaching.

'I think no matter what field you're in: work, music or art, you can learn something from everybody. The kids say stuff and you learn from it. The other day, they were asked: 'What do you want to be when you grow up?' A load of them were saying soccer players. One of them just said: 'I just want a simple life, because that's a happy life.' It was like: 'My God."

However, Veale will soon put everything else aside and switch to full-time training. Events such as the European Cup and the World University Games are on the horizon, while the start of the Tokyo 2020 Olympics is less than 500 days away. To secure qualification, Veale will need to be ranked among the world's top 60.

'I'm definitely not where I was before and where I want to be,' she says. 'I still have a hip issue going on that I had before, so that's probably my major concern at the moment, getting that right. That's a big thing for me. When I got pregnant, it made it worse again. It's just one of those things I have to manage.

'Winning a national title, it's brilliant, you can never take it for granted. But I want to see the bigger picture. I don't want to just win a national title. The Olympics are the pinnacle of what we're all aiming for next year. In the meantime, we have a lot of big races coming up before then.

'Rob was 35 winning World Championships. Olive Loughnane was 31 at her best when she won in Berlin. So I am lucky that I have time on my side.'

The life of an elite athlete is rarely straightforward though. To pursue her dream, Veale needs to make a number of sacrifices and must also rely heavily on the support of others.

'I still live with my parents. Athletics isn't a sport where you're going to get a lot of money unless you're at the very top, and now that I'm climbing to the top, if I wasn't living at home, I'd be lost. I'm just literally in from training now and my dad was out on the bike with me, so he was doing my gels, my drinks, my timing and keeping the wind off me. I got too hot then, I had to take off my jacket and my headband, so it's doing so many different things at once. And listening to me cursing when the session gets hard and having to deal with me.

'There are times after training like the other day, I came in, I had a hard session and just took off my gear. I threw everything onto the floor and literally just went to bed. I didn't have the energy to pick up my gear, so my poor mother had to deal with that as well.'

Fianna, meanwhile, is now four years old and unsurprisingly, is already looking like following in her mother's footsteps.

'I'm not even asking or telling her to do anything, but I come in and she's like: 'I want to do my training now.' So it's out on the road with her and run a bit and come back. Or she's copying me doing my stretches and exercises. It's just [repeating] what they see obviously. It's gas how it's happening again [like it did with my dad and me].'

Veale says her mental health remains a work in progress. The West Waterford AC athlete continues to regularly see a sports psychologist. She acknowledges her message of 'it's okay not to feel okay' may sound 'cheesy' or clichéd, but that should not detract from its importance.

'I'm a deep thinker I suppose and now that I've come out the other end, I just want people to know that they can [get better]. I would have thought I'm never going to come out of this stage. Even in terms of a career, I thought I won't even get a job, I won't do athletics, I'll just be this person in hospital for the rest of my life. It's not that way at all now, it's really not.

'Rob even, I would have thought he was so hardy and never went through any shit. Now I know he did and everyone has.

'It's okay to ask for help and it will be normal to go through the hard times. [Success] doesn't keep going up and up. When you have the adversity and the bad days, it's about getting over those things and simply expecting them.'

Statistics have shown that Irish people tend to drop out of their chosen sport in their late teens at an alarming rate amid the transition from school to college, and these figures relate particularly to females. For a long time, it seemed as if Veale too would succumb to this unfortunate trend.

'In Ireland, the culture we have, you're thinking you're missing out on parties and college life. I would have used drink as a crutch. You feel alright for the night and then you're back to the way you were feeling again the next day with depression, anxiety and stuff.

'Being fit, powerful, putting your body on the line and being out there, pushing yourself to the limit, there's no better feeling.

'I want to get to the next Olympics and will try as hard as I can, but I'm going to enjoy this journey and take the risk and what happens happens.

'It's exciting. It's like there's joy in misery and pain and suffering. It's finding what's worth suffering for. And we all have something — it could be music or art or whatever.

'There'll be a good few shocked friends [reading this article], but that's good, because it's real and it helps people in this fake [social media] world.

'Someone was messing with me recently saying: 'Wouldn't you love to just be a simple girl who is happy with their normal life?' They probably are the happiest and they don't even think about these things. A lot of the time, it's people who are striving to be successful [who are at risk of depression]. And in the end, they're the ones that will suffer, the ones that are putting the pressure on themselves and who have that mindset.

'I wouldn't be the fittest-looking on the start line, but that soul and heart and passion, when I get that mindset, I'm just so driven and dogged. It's funny how your mind can be your greatest thing ever, and also your worst thing. So it's about getting that balance.'

NINE

THE OLD MAN AND THE CLUB

—

FINTAN O'TOOLE | 16 MARCH

BEFORE LOOKING FORWARD to tomorrow, he can look back to when it all began. Donie Sheahan maps out his itinerary for the weekend. He will board a train today from Killarney, land in Dublin where he'll be collected by his daughter and base himself in the capital.

For a starter he'll be watching the footage from Tralee later as Kerry and Mayo square off before the main course of his sporting weekend tomorrow afternoon. Dr Crokes make their latest assault on a national title against Galway's Corofin.

The patron of the Kerry club will lend his support, a figure who provides a neat symmetry between the 2019 All-Ireland club instalment and the original version back in 1971 when he coached East Kerry, the maiden victors and the only divisional team to have achieved that honour.

In the interim he acclaimed the Dr Crokes breakthrough in 1992, savoured their return to that summit two years ago and is profoundly grateful to be witnessing their bid for a third All-Ireland crown.

'I'll be 93 in April, the same day as the Queen of England. She'll be 93 as well. The 21st of April 1926, I was born.

'The one thing I'll say is I didn't drink or smoke all my life, I'd say 'twas a help. I kept working all my life. I'd an interest in everything.

'And I'm very lucky, I've people and my family organising for me. To be going up to an All-Ireland final now with my club, it's a big thing. I thought '92 was the end of it and now here I am.'

Before there were recognisable club heavyweights, TG4 cameras documenting every step through the winter and the doors of Croke Park being opened up on St Patrick's Day, the grassroots game lived in a different world.

The clamour for club All-Irelands to be introduced grew louder in the 1960s. Provinces took matters into their own hands in organising meetings between county champions and by the 1970 GAA Congress, there were two motions on the agenda from Galway and Wexford looking for an official national competition. The vote swung 92-74 in favour of All-Ireland recognition for clubs.

If the thorny issue of GAA fixtures continues to generate a feverish debate, consider the schedule in 1971. In the spring East Kerry won a Munster final against Cork's Muskerry before they were placed in cold storage until 5 September.

In a year where Offaly lifted Sam Maguire, Gracefield flew the Faithful flag in that All-Ireland semi-final but East Kerry prevailed by five points and then struck five goals against Down's Bryansford in the final. Croke Park was the setting on Sunday 21 November but the win was greeted with little fanfare as outlined by Murt Galvin, the Kerry county treasurer at the time in Jack Mahon's book 'For Love Of Town And Village'.

'When we arrived back that night in Killarney at about 11.30pm, there were two people at the railway station, the father of one of the players and the player's brother. Coming home that night we might as well have been out playing a club game in Duhallow or Rathmore.'

Listowel native Sheahan marvels at the explosion in stature since.

'I never thought it would come to be such a good competition. I thought there was only once or twice they'd have it but they deserve great credit for it.

'There's lads there winning All-Irelands in Croke Park and who could you win it better than with your own fellas? There's great pride in it.'

He can cherish that East Kerry victory, the products of five clubs blended together to make a formidable outfit. They stitched together a local three-in-a-row between 1968 and 1970, conquerors of a South Kerry team who had a famed figure in their ranks.

'You see, we beat Waterville in three county finals.

'And I'd always say to [Mick O'] Dwyer, 'Three-in-a-row, Mike'.

"Ah, shag you,' he'd say. 'Ye had the pick of the county.'

'True but I had to put them together. They were there three years in a row in the final, the last time we beat them was close now alright. Dwyer always maintains he should have got a penalty. But I thought it was no penalty anyway.'

They only got one shot at All-Ireland glory and seized it. Divisional sides were soon exempt from competing as it became the preserve of the clubs.

'We'd have won more I think. We'd a great team. We were

giving four or five to Kerry at the time, we'd great players like Mick Gleeson, Dan Kavanagh, Pat Moynihan. If the players weren't Kerry seniors, they were Kerry juniors.

'I had the two best fellas ever behind me. There was Brendy Walsh, chairman of the board, he was from Glenflesk and he was a great organiser.

'And Denis Fenton was out from Spa there, he was the best secretary I ever met. Now that's his nephew Brian that's playing for Dublin at the moment. He's a very good footballer, very good.

'Brendy I suppose must have asked me to train the team. I knew Dr Eamonn [O'Sullivan] well, he was the trainer of Kerry, I learned from him.

'He used give me a formula to make up an old bottle for the team, as a rub for my own fellas. There was no physios then. I mostly fixed them up myself. It was different times. We plodded away anyway.'

His affection for that winning class of 1971 is clear. One player, Weeshie Fogarty, would go on to provide the voice that chronicled the feats of Kerry teams for years, finding a natural home in the radio gantry. He passed away last November, a week before Dr Crokes lifted a Munster title.

'Weeshie would talk the leg off a pot of course! Ah but he was a fine fella. I was Crokes and he was Legion but we were the best of friends.

'They were all great friends of mine. A lot of them are dead, I mean it's sad for the likes of me. I do miss them, chatting about football and that.'

If he had been a foe of Mick O'Dwyer's on the club scene in Kerry, their careers would soon intersect to see them work side by side.

'In '75 I was one of the fellas elected [as Kerry selector] and Dwyer was elected. Dwyer had a meeting and said he'd train the team and we all agreed. That's how he started. It was a lot of running. I always think of Dwyer in '75 and he said there was only one way we'd beat Dublin and that was if we were fitter than them.

'I worked with him for about three years. You'd thrash out before the match whatever it was. In '75 I met him the morning of the final in the hotel. I was saying if a fella gets hurt, who'll we bring in. He said Ger O'Driscoll from Valentia and I agreed with that. Anyway when Mickey Ned [O'Sullivan] got knocked out, Dwyer called in Ger and he got a goal and a point.

'Dwyer was cool and tough. He never got ruffled. They were great rivals that time, Kerry and Dublin. There's a son now of Tony Hanahoe's, he's working with my son above in Vincent's Hospital in Dublin. It's amazing that you come across fellas after.'

They supervised the Kerry U21 side in 1975 as well, a collection of players that would go on to be such dominant forces in the sport. Scan an eye over that star-studded teamsheet and the surnames leap off the page — Nelligan, Ó Sé, Kennelly, Spillane, Walsh, Sheehy, Moran, Doyle and O'Shea.

Sheahan spent three years in Kerry senior dressing rooms. They discovered gems in different ways around the county.

'I'll tell you how we found the Bomber. The chairman of the Beale club was a fella called John Francis Aherne. I knew him well.

'That time to be elected for a selector, you had to go around and meet the clubs and get voted by the clubs. So I was out canvassing one winter and I met John Francis. I said, 'Have ye any fella?'

'Then he said, 'We've a fella, they call him the Bomber.' I said to send him in. Now he was a big, strong, awkward man. But by God, he went down to Waterville for 12 months and Dwyer definitely made a footballer out of him down there.

'We'd have debated in '77 whether we'd play him or not. We didn't play him but we did in '78 and that was the start of him, he got three goals [in the final against Dublin]. He was a big active fella and had a great football brain.'

Another player from that part of North Kerry has been in his thoughts from earlier.

'Ogie [Moran] was in Rinn in the Irish college with my lads when he was younger. One of them came back, I don't know was it Liam or Kieran, and told me there's a fella called Ogie Moran and he's a great footballer. And when I became a selector, I had him in the back of my mind the whole time.'

Those were chapters in Sheahan's GAA tale but the overarching theme revolves around Dr Crokes. He settled in Kerry after a circuitous route around the country. Work as a chemist kept him on the move, but wherever he landed the GAA was a comfortable outlet to slip into.

'I worked in Thurles for nearly a year. I was into football naturally. I tried to get an old junior team going there in Thurles Sarsfields. The one thing they were interested in was hurling.

'And from there I went up to Dunleer in Louth. I played with St Mary's of Ardee, they'd some great players for Louth like Paddy Markey. One day the Mary's represented Louth in the O'Byrne Cup, they were that good. They were mad for football, like myself.'

He opened the doors of Sheahan's Pharmacy in Killarney in 1953. It's still going on 34 Main Street under the running of his son Liam. They expanded in Kenmare with another son Paul opening a pharmacy there in 1994.

'I got a job in Killarney first, I was dispensing the medicine in two hospitals and the county home as well. I knew a lot of the patients, they were fine fellas. The nurses were great, looking after them.'

He had been roped in to play for Dr Crokes for a summer in 1946, fell back in with the club when he returned in the 50s and has never left.

'I was around 20 years chairman. My wife used to say to me every year, 'Did you give up?' But sure at the AGM, every fella would be saying that I was doing a great job and no fella wanted the bloody job. One year finishing up, I talked Tom Long into taking it over. I stayed on as the delegate of the county board for nearly 50 years.'

His mind is crammed with rich football tales that tumble out. That seismic win for Dr Crokes in 1992 against Dublin's Thomas Davis.

'An official went to stop me from going down and they were getting the cup in the Hogan Stand. I shoved him out of my bloody way. I was excited. You do things that you wouldn't do normally. Ah to see the Crokes win in Croke Park was great.'

The corner-forward that day is now in the control room, expertly pulling the levers to ensure the Dr Crokes trophy cabinet has been heaving in recent years.

'I see Pat [O'Shea] there could get 30 fellas out a few days after Christmas to go out training. There's no one else who'd get that. He's a great trainer and he has great command. He's respected by the players, they think highly of him.

'He's no nonsense. I remember one day we were above after beating The Rock [Austin Stacks] in the final of the county league. I went in to congratulate the lads because I knew a lot of them and Pat was inside and he was making a show about all the mistakes they'd made. He has high standards.'

After 1992, Dr Crokes only managed one county senior triumph in the next 18 seasons.

But the autumn of 2010 kick-started an era that has left Sheahan marvelling. Since his 84th birthday he has seen a title collection comprising seven in Kerry and five in Munster along with national treks to see games against Armagh, Dublin, Mayo, Galway, Derry and Longford opponents.

The 2017 All-Ireland was special for Sheahan in seeing the Dr Crokes goalscorer that day get his moment of club joy.

'I was delighted for the Gooch, I put my arms around him above in Croke Park that day. He's one of the best I've ever seen. He's a great football brain, he's in the right spot at the right time. He can do amazing things.

'If he was below there in the bank years ago and a fella came into me wanting to meet the Gooch. I could walk down to the bank and he would be upstairs and he'd come down to me and shake hands with whoever. A great man that way.'

As we talk in a small room at the back of the pharmacy, he is regularly switching his gaze to monitor the Saturday afternoon running at Gowran Park and Sandown Park. This week was never just about the GAA clubs finals, Cheltenham always set to command his interest as he hoped Willie Mullins could end his pursuit of the Gold Cup.

Horse racing has always been a passion. He sent For William to the Kerry Grand National in Listowel and finished second twice. For Bill gave him many afternoons in the limelight, a victor under Davy Russell at the Fairyhouse Easter Festival in 2010.

'I used to go to Cheltenham when it was only a two-day meeting. There's a big meeting there in November and I had one [Dromhale Lady in 1998] there alright and I was beaten in a photo finish by a horse called Lady Rebecca, I'll always think of it, and she went and won nine races after.

'[Michael] Hourigan used to train for me at the time and I'd a runner in a big National Hunt trial stake above at Punchestown one time and we won. Robert Hall was interviewing the two of us after the race and he said, 'I suppose there'll be big celebrations Michael after this?'

'Says Hourigan, 'Well I'll tell you, Donie has the free travel and he came up on the train, and Donie's going home on the train and I drove up and I'm going home in my car. So that'll be the celebrations. And he was right, that was it!

'I was very lucky, I'd a lot of very good horses. I enjoy Cheltenham a lot.'

Home is on the Lewis Road just across from Fitzgerald Stadium.

'They all say to me if I could I'd have built inside in the stadium! It was pure fluke, I got a site there. I'm at the front of the Crokes as well, I walk around the corner and I'm into the pitch.

'Liam, my son, was secretary of the stadium and I was treasurer for a bit and I was stuck a lot in the stadium.'

Anytime there is a match in the Killarney venue he ventures over, slipping into the press box to watch on. He has five children,

13 grandchildren and three great grandchildren. His family and football have always consumed him and kept him active.

'It's been a great interest all my life and I've met a pile of friends and a pile of people. My wife [Carmel] often said there's nothing in the house but football and horses. And I always said to her I can't dispute that!

'Football was always like a drug for me I suppose. I never thought I'd live to see the day the Crokes club on their own would win an All-Ireland club. Well I did in 1992 and again two years ago. I'm hoping I can see it a third time.'

Forty-eight years on from his first trip, he's back on the All-Ireland club final trail.

—

TEN

LOOKING DOWN ON LEANNE

—

EMMA DUFFY | 4 MAY

A PARENT'S PRIDE in their child is something special.

It's pretty much the first thing that both John and Ita Kiernan, parents of Ireland and West Ham star Leanne, mention as they begin to speak glowingly of their youngest daughter.

Leanne and her siblings really are their pride and joy.

* * *

It's Wednesday afternoon, just after two o'clock when John's mobile rings.

But this isn't just any Wednesday afternoon in the Kiernan household in Bailieborough, County Cavan. It's the Wednesday afternoon before the 2019 Women's FA Cup final, in which Leanne will line out in Wembley Stadium against Manchester City — for whom her Ireland team-mate Megan Campbell plies her trade.

This is the biggest game of 20-year-old Kiernan's glittering career so far, and it's only fitting that we go back to where it all began and rewind to earlier days and to those closest to her. Those who have always been there through the ups and downs, the highs and lows, the good days and the bad.

It's all come around pretty fast, after all.

* * *

The baby of the house, much of Leanne's childhood was spent with a ball at her feet, and with her three siblings. While it soon became apparent that she had something very special, life growing up in Cavan was nothing out of the ordinary: school, knocking around the family pig farm, and trying her hand at any sport that came her way dominated her daily life.

Soccer wasn't exactly on her radar from early doors; Gaelic football with the local club in Bailieborough and athletics for Shercock AC were the main two before she found her true calling. The real memory John has though was the fact that she carried a football everywhere she went.

'From six or seven, a very young age, she always had a ball,' he smiles. 'Everywhere she went, she was always kicking a ball. When she'd go and visit her cousins she'd bring the ball in the car. She was always like that.

'She was in Shercock at the running but she loved the Gaelic as well. It was always there. She was into all sorts of sports. Very active and always running, out and about. Gaelic was a big part of it. She played underage here in Bailieborough and she enjoyed it.'

Bailieborough Shamrocks started the club up in 2008, and Tony O'Reilly has fond memories of coaching Kiernan there and at county level. Such was her outstanding talent that she was playing for the U12s at the age of just nine.

A four-time Ulster club juvenile cross-country champion and a remarkably fast sprinter, Leanne's athletics background really helped on the Gaelic pitch too.

'We used to play her inside, her pace was great,' O'Reilly recalls. 'With the soccer, she'd be dribbling the ball along the ground, I'd be giving out to her... 'Pick it up to fuck! Next thing she'd bury it in the net, and what could you say then?

'She had a great awareness, she had a great burst inside. She had lightning pace and we used to try and isolate her. She was full of confidence and she'd do the unexpected with a ball. She was buzzing with confidence. She was just outstanding.'

He tells brilliant stories from Community Games to Féile, to the first year of the John Egan tournament in which the side played in Fitzgerald Stadium in Killarney. She also graced Croke Park for a half-time game with the Cavan schools.

Two years of playing county with the U14s soon followed, but that coincided with her star rising more and more on the soccer scene.

* * *

A five-a-side game in her first year of secondary school was the first time Leanne properly played soccer. It was crystal clear from day one though that she was prodigiously talented. From there, she went to the nearby Kingscourt Harps where she played with the boys, and ran rings around them week on week in the North East Counties Schoolboys League (NECSL).

Despite being extremely small in stature at the time, she soon made the Ulster U15 schoolgirls squad and was fast-tracked to the senior women's team at Kingscourt where she starred around the middle for a brief period.

But soon after that, the FAI emerging talent programme came calling as she shone at the Gaynor Cup and elsewhere, and she made the switch to Shelbourne at 15. As bigger and better things came thick and fast, any other sports soon had to be knocked on the head.

John remembers an Ulster minor final, in which Bailieborough amalgamated with Knockbride to form Eastern Gaels and won, as the turning point.

'There was some trial for the Irish U16s at the time and she couldn't go to the Ulster final,' he says. 'I'd say that was the first time that there was a clash. After that, she stayed away from the Gaelic altogether. She couldn't do them both, there wasn't time with all the commitment.'

At a formative stage in her teenage years, all of the sport was brilliant for Leanne. She absolutely loved it, but not only that, it helped her in more ways than one could imagine.

Leanne was, in fact, coming to terms with something much more difficult than making a decision between soccer and Gaelic football. She was learning to deal with grief and loss.

* * *

While the Kiernans are synonymous with farming, the family were also big into rallying. Their two sons, Patrick and Gary, were mad into it — Gary still is — and it was a huge part of life at home.

Leanne and Laura, as the younger sisters, were in awe of the two lads — Leanne, in particular. Ita shares priceless memories of Patrick, the eldest, rallying Leanne around the piggery every evening. She was only eight or nine at the time, but the joy on her face every time said it all.

Despite the age gap and the fact that she was the youngest and he was the eldest, the pair were as thick as thieves. And while Patrick, or Paddy as he was called by many, tried his hardest to get Leanne away from the football and into the rallying, she stood firm.

The Kiernans' world fell apart in July 2013 when Patrick was killed in a car accident.

He was just 23.

'Our son Patrick is looking down on Leanne now this weekend,' Ita says as she breaks down over the phone. 'Hopefully…'

This is about much more than football.

'She was very close to him. She has him in her locket around her neck over in England. I'm delighted…'

You can sense just how difficult it is for Ita to open up. And how difficult it has been through the years. But this really is more than just football for the family.

Through the dark days, it was the shining light. Ita jokes that John is Leanne's agent, but truth be told he is, and was, through those endless hours of driving up and down to Shelbourne when she made the big switch.

Her progression brought comfort and hope through the family's struggle.

* * *

The 180km round-trip to Dublin was done three or four times a week, leaving straight after school at 5pm and not landing home until 11pm with a two-hour session in between.

'Even when we went to Dublin first, they used to slag her because she brought the ball with her,' John laughs, picking up on earlier. Old habits die hard.

'She'd get out of the car for training but she'd have her own ball with her.'

On top of the sheer amount of driving and the intense training, there was the fact that even the two weekday evenings she wasn't in the capital, she had strength and conditioning work to fulfil at home. When it came to that stage, there was no time for anything other than soccer.

The bit of school had to be done of course, but her Leaving Cert year was when she well and truly made her breakthrough.

From a hat-trick in the Women's FAI Cup final at the Aviva Stadium to announcing herself on the international stage in style, the list goes on when you look back at how amazing 2016 was on an individual level.

Her stellar performances with the Irish U19s and with the double champions brought a senior international call-up — and a goal on her debut — as her meteoric rise continued.

On that, Ita is keen to say a big thank you to Sue Ronan, the manager who handed Leanne her first start, which was a memorable one.

She'll go the whole way, as Ronan said many times.

'She used to go and watch her when she was playing for Shelbourne and she had her picked for the Irish squad,' Ita explains. 'She played under her for another few games and then she retired. It's great. I'm delighted it worked out for Sue.

'She saw something in Leanne. She was pleased that she had picked her up before her time leaving. I'm delighted that Leanne worked out for her.'

* * *

As she excelled, and broke down more and more barriers, talk of crossing the pond arose.

After completing her Leaving Cert, Leanne earned a place in Ballyhaise Agricultural College where she continued her education and pursued her love for farming. The opportunity to follow her dream of playing football professionally was one she couldn't turn down, and when West Ham came knocking, it was a no-brainer.

'I remember at Shelbourne, she talked about different clubs, different universities,' John recalls, 'and at the time she said to me, 'Look, I'd like to go over and have a look'. I said, 'Yeah, just tell me whatever day and I'll fly over'.

'We went to have a look at their facilities and she had a good feeling about them.

'Since she went over she's been very happy. That was the biggest surprise we got. We thought she'd be homesick but never has been for one minute.

'Look, it's all worked out for the best. We're very happy and very proud of her. Hopefully it keeps going well for her.'

That's been quite a surprise to those that know her: that she settled in so quickly to life in London. A homebird through and through before now, she's taken it all in her stride and fits in seamlessly.

While she does miss the farming dearly, John is confident that she'll be home over the summer to work on the land with the pigs. She needs to keep in touch, he says, despite the fact that she's living the dream across the water.

'Our advice to her would have been to try and follow it to the best you possibly can,' her father adds. 'She can come back and finish her education then at a later time.

'She might as well pursue it and see where it takes her. No different to any other parent, they want their child to be happy and that's all we were interested in really.

'West Ham have treated her really well and she's very happy with them. They're like a family. She's very happy, we can't believe how happy she is there. We appreciate everything that's done for her, it's been very good.'

And his wife echoes his words over and over, her pride in her daughter bursting through.

'I'm delighted for Leanne that it's worked out well for her,' she smiles. 'That everything else went her way and she's happy.

'She's happy, that's all that counts at the end of the day. No matter what she's doing, she's happy. We're delighted for her, delighted. And West Ham is very good to her, very good. We couldn't ask for any more, it's brilliant.'

* * *

The Hammers have had a superb first season in the Women's Super League and today, they'll round it off with a first-ever FA Cup final appearance against Manchester City in Wembley.

Leanne has been one of the stars of the show throughout

their season — her debut one over there — and despite missing a stint through injury, she's back to her brilliant best once again and banging in the goals.

Thankfully, Ita and John have been there to see plenty of them — as well as Gary and Laura — travelling over three times a month or so.

'We go over to a lot of games and it's a good interest for us as well,' John enthuses.

'We've had a lot of very good days going to matches, and we're very proud of what she's doing. She's progressed so much. The way I look at it is she's on a learning curve. She's learning loads at West Ham, she's learning loads with Ireland.'

They've been over the last two Sundays in a row, leaving Cavan bright and early, flying over that morning for the match and returning the same night. Sure it's as handy as going down the country for a game at this stage.

'We love to see her progression. But the main thing for us was she had to be happy. If she wasn't happy, she wouldn't have stayed there. That was a big thing. She's very happy, and long may it last. If it stays like that and she's injury free, Jesus, I think she'll go further.'

Ita takes over, explaining her hatred of flying before now, and how much she's turned that around and absolutely loves their near-weekly visits.

'I dreaded it. I couldn't nearly go on holidays if I had to fly. I started and now I can't be got off a plane!

'Three or four times in the month and we're away. We love to see the games.

'The girls treat us like we're their mother and father too because we're over all the time. The other girls are from

America and that so their parents wouldn't get over at all. We're treated as family to them, to all the lassies. It's great.'

'If you don't know these two, you mustn't know me,' Leanne posted on Instagram earlier this week alongside pictures with the pair.

Ita also tells of how the family recently gifted her an iPad that's been an absolute godsend, her glowing personality coming through more and more with every story.

'The iPad, I'm keeping it busy now,' she grins. 'They bought me it for Christmas and they're mad now. They said we should have kept it in the shop, the head's buried in it! It's great. FaceTime, social media and everything. It feels like she's with you all the time at home, that she's not away at all. It's brilliant.'

* * *

With a group of 30 family and close friends heading over for the big game, thankfully the iPad won't be needed on this occasion. Gary and Laura unfortunately can't make the journey this time around, but with all of the action live on BBC, they'll be glued to it.

'A big occasion for Leanne and for us all, for everyone,' Ita beams. That it is. It's huge.

And Leanne is ready for their invasion, with plenty of Kiernan 8 jerseys ready for her nearest and dearest, who flew out yesterday.

'We wouldn't miss it,' John assures, as himself and his wife gear up to lead the way. 'It'll be a great occasion.'

Leanne's footballing exploits have most definitely kept them going through the years, so how great would this be to put the cherry on top. She's given them enough incredible days in her two decades thus far, but what about this, on the biggest stage possible.

A slight step up from Fitzgerald Stadium, John and Ita share their excitement to see Wembley in the flesh and everything that goes hand-in-hand with the occasion.

With the attendance record set at over 45,000 last year, 52,000 tickets had been sold and distributed mid-week so that bodes well for the crowd Leanne will strut her stuff in front of at the iconic venue this evening.

But all that really counts at the end of the day is her beloved parents — two of the most important people in her life — watching on from the stands, her brother and sister tuning in to the television, and her guardian angel Patrick looking down from above.

Each and every step of the way.

ELEVEN

LORD AND MASTER

—

AS JODY MORGAN made his way down from high in the Tavern Stand, weaving his way through the wildly frenzied celebrations amid the noise and unsolicited drama of it all, and into the famous Lord's Pavilion, it all came flooding back.

It may have only taken him a couple of minutes to get from one of the players' boxes to the pitch, but he could have squeezed two decades worth of memories into that short walk.

The emotion, the hurt, the difficult days, the 'shit' thrown at his son and their family down through the years, but, above all, he was bursting with pride, remembering the magical moments in Saint Catherine's housing estate in Rush, when they first embarked on this journey.

His son was now a World Cup-winning captain.

Jody waited patiently, along with the rest of the families, for the players to complete their lap of honour and then, maybe 20 minutes after England wicket-keeper Jos Buttler had broken the bails to hand England the Cricket World Cup,

Eoin appeared, medal around his neck, carrying the trophy.

No words can do that moment — between father and son — justice.

'We didn't speak, we just hugged… because we know,' an emotional Morgan says.

'We had been texting during the week and had this thing. We just kept saying to each other, 'We're nearly there.' Throughout the tournament, that's all we said: 'We're nearly there.'

'I texted Eoin before the final to say how proud we were of him and just how good he has been. Yesterday, he just said: 'We did this, Dad, me and you.' He doesn't say very much but when he says it, he means it.'

Jody Morgan, as he had done for the majority of the World Cup, watched every ball of a final for the ages as if he was out in the middle himself. As if he was still out in Kenure Park captaining the Rush 3rd XI, just as he had done when a four-year-old Eoin first strapped on the pads.

'I still can't really believe it,' he continues. 'It's probably only sinking in today. You start to lose it a little bit in the moment because it brings up emotions about Rush and all the things that happened in Irish cricket. I don't even know what airport I'm flying home from.'

Morgan, oftentimes with different members of the family including Eoin's mother Olivia, has travelled back and across from Dublin for all but one of England's games en route to the Promised Land, living and breathing every moment of a rollercoaster eight-week tournament.

They decided to skip the semi-final victory over Australia last week, purely because 'we wouldn't put ourselves through that again', after bearing witness to a couple of England defeats during the first phase, which left the host nation's hopes hanging by a thread.

'We spoke after the Sri Lanka match [that England lost], and by God, I wasn't too pleased about some of that, but we spoke about different things,' Morgan explains.

'I normally wouldn't bring it up when they've lost but you just get a bit carried away. Eoin just reminded me it was a long tournament and was so calm. He handles me well, he handles everybody well.

'Even when I'm not there, I'm always there and he knows that. Myself and Olivia didn't go to the semi-final and didn't even watch the second half on TV. We had to turn everything off until it was over, but he knows we're there.

'After that win, I just text him: "We're nearly there," and thank God, yesterday they got there. It's hard to put into words.'

In lifting the World Cup trophy aloft at Lord's, the Home of Cricket, Eoin Morgan has now been placed on a pedestal with legendary England captains such as Martin Johnson and Bobby Moore, leading his team to sporting immortality.

Already one of cricket's pre-eminent batsmen and leaders, the victory over New Zealand was a life and career-defining moment for the 32-year-old, whose talents were first honed in north county Dublin and his character and personality built at home and in the classrooms of Catholic University School on Leeson Street.

Strong-willed, ambitious, focused and a prodigious talent, Morgan knew where he was going from a young age. He made no secret of his desire to reach the top, and growing up in a country that could not offer a career in professional cricket, he had to look elsewhere.

'That was as hard on his family as it was on him as well. It wasn't easy,' Jody says.

After playing 63 times for Ireland, it was perhaps predictable that his transition into England colours a decade ago was not accepted among some quarters on this island, and even to this day, it is an issue of great disagreement.

It has meant Morgan, and his family, have never been able to escape criticism, and there were times when he received it from both sides, particularly when he wouldn't sing the English national anthem.

Even still, through the peaks and troughs, Morgan remained stubbornly committed. A tenacious desire to succeed drove him on, and nothing was going to get in his way.

'His brothers and sisters knew from the word go he'd make it,' Jody continues. 'His capacity to be able to keep everything in his head and be calm. He got that from school in CUS. The vice-principal, Kevin Jennings, he'd always say, 'Tell him to be calm no matter what.'

'And there was a lot of shit thrown at him, especially in 2015 after that World Cup and it was a very low ebb for him and being left off the Test team was a huge blow to Eoin. He's had all that but he has a great capacity to come back from all that.

'The joy on his face yesterday evening, it wasn't 'look what I've done or look at me'.

'He lets his cricket do the talking. He doesn't get carried away about anything, whether it's good or bad, and that's stood to him. It's a very special trait to have.'

Just as he has done as England captain, Morgan has always carried the responsibility on his shoulders comfortably. He never got distracted by the nationality argument in the background, nor those who questioned his patriotism.

Last summer, he returned to Rush for a mini-documentary commissioned by the England and Wales Cricket Board [ECB] charting his rise from a housing estate in Fingal to one of the most high-profile positions in the sport.

As a kid, Morgan would spend hours playing cricket with his five siblings on a concrete strip beside his house, adopting his father's, grandfather's and great grandfather's love of the sport. He has always been aware of that heritage, of that family history, Jody says.

When the Morgan family relocated to Santry after Jody was appointed as the head groundsman of the Trinity Sports Complex, where the Dublin footballers and hurlers used to train, a 13-year-old Eoin switched cricket clubs, joining Malahide, and earned a scholarship to CUS.

Shortly after yesterday's final, former Dublin footballer Paul Clarke recalled on Twitter how Eoin Morgan used to collect balls during their training sessions during the summer of 1995, the year the Boys in Blue lifted the Sam Maguire.

'He would have played hurling, he would have played Gaelic football, he would have played rugby,' Jody says. 'But cricket was always the one.

'It makes it all the more satisfying for me. My father left us cricket, nothing else. We never had anything.

'It's a great story. Kevin Jennings at CUS is responsible for it. Dublin GAA, they changed our lives when we moved to Santry.

'That facilitated Eoin's success to a certain degree, it gave me the security of work and I then had the time to go with him. Sometimes when I was meant to be working, I was at cricket with Eoin.

'I got a call from Keith Barr this morning, John Costello last night, all of the people that have facilitated Eoin and all of the people that have facilitated us in turn.'

The hope now is that Eoin Morgan will bring the World Cup trophy back to Rush.

'He's a proud Irishman,' Jody adds. 'Even way before a World Cup or anything like that, I used to say just be careful what we say because I would see him coming back to coach Ireland in time, and he would say 'yeah'.

'He'd never close the door on anything. I would see him in that capacity in years to come, and I hope I live to see it.

'There is nothing I would love better than to see him play in Dublin, or in any part of Ireland, and there would be nobody more pleased if Eoin brought the World Cup trophy back to Rush to celebrate. It would be some homecoming, yeah.'

TWELVE

THE ROCKY ROAD

—

AARON GALLAGHER | 11 MAY

IT ALL HAPPENED in the blink of an eye, but Christy McElligott can still remember with precise detail the day that would change his life forever.

'I was heading to Wexford at about four in the morning,' he recalls. 'An articulated truck came round the bend, jack-knifed, lost control and hit the truck I was travelling to work in. Head on. Took my leg clean off.

'It was grand at the time. I say 'grand', but by that I mean I didn't feel any pain. The leg was completely severed off me below the knee. I remember I had a pair of these Adidas button-up tracksuit bottoms and they came flying off too. I was left in my boxers.'

He pauses for a moment, smiling. 'I actually found it funny when I thought about it afterwards: I was embarrassed that I was just left in a pair of boxer shorts.

'I tried to get out through the passenger door, but it was wedged against the side of a ditch. So I had to kick the windscreen of my truck out with my left leg and throw myself out onto the ground. The two trucks were on fire at the time, so I had to crawl along the ground on my backside, crawl backwards to safety.

'I got up once or twice to try and hop; I hopped two or three feet and went down on the ground again, because I was exhausted. I felt exhausted, but that was because I was losing so much blood.'

The summer of 2001 was drawing to a close and McElligott had just six weeks beforehand reached the pinnacle of his career. It was that rare, blissful moment in a footballer's life when sporting excellence, magnificent achievement and local pride all came together into one.

He was 30 years old at the time and with a successful League of Ireland career under his belt, one which included a Premier Division title with St Patrick's Athletic in 1996 under Brian Kerr, an FAI Cup runners-up medal the same season and having also become Monaghan United's most expensive ever signing.

Actually starting out his footballing career as a highly-talented young goalkeeper before later making his name as a striker, he was even offered the opportunity to go on trial with Manchester United in the late 1980s during his teens.

After his two-year spell at Monaghan at the end of the '90s, though, he returned to his local side to see out the twilight years of his career. The place where it all began — Ballymun United. Winning the FAI Junior Cup in 2001 was the absolute peak, he says.

Having proudly grown up in the flats, bringing that trophy back to share with his neighbours, his family and his friends, meant more than any other piece of silverware ever could. It might be difficult to understand placing so much emphasis on an amateur title, but it was true. It was truly, truly special.

It might have been just an FAI Junior Cup to those on the outside, but to those who did recognise its significance, it represented the culmination of years of hard work, a tight-knit community coming together, and a bond between local lads who had grown up through good times and bad prevailing, succeeding, winning together side-by-side as brothers.

The entire area rallied around the team on their journey to the final at Tolka Park in 2001. Supporters adopted David Gray's hit song 'Babylon' (substituting in the lyric Ballymun instead) as their anthem and would even enjoy an open-top bus tour in the summer sunshine to celebrate afterwards.

McElligott, striker and skipper, captained Ballymun to their 3-0 victory against St Kevin's — that Junior Cup being the fourth title his side won in a magnificent quadruple year where the north Dublin club enjoyed a historic clean sweep.

But less than two months after that crowning moment of joy and euphoria achieved with the friends he had grown up alongside all those years ago, the former League of Ireland star's life was turned upside down in an instant.

'Somebody crashed their car into the back of the chap's truck who had hit me,' he says, picking up the story. 'That person must have saw me lying on the ground after I crawled out of my lorry and they rang the ambulance.

'This stranger, I can't remember if it was a man or a woman, came down and lifted me up under the arms and tried to carry me back to safety. But they put me back down and got sick everywhere because of the sight of my right leg.

'Every time they tried to pull me backwards the flames from the two trucks were coming with them. It was a scary time and I always remember thinking to myself: 'Please don't let me die in the countryside all on my own.' I thought I was going to die, but in a weird way it was kind of peaceful. There was no pain at all with my leg, I just got more and more tired and felt like I wanted to go asleep.

'It felt like a couple of seconds,' he says, before snapping his fingers suddenly. 'Then there were these luminous green jackets around me — the ambulance people. They put me in the back of the ambulance and drove me to Limerick.

'They brought me to the hospital,' he continues, 'stabilised me, sent me to Waterford Regional, and my family came down.

'Before they operated — the doctors had to cut above the knee because bacteria was after getting into the area and infected it — they gave me a consent form. I remember my mam standing beside me, saying there was no other alternative, that they would have to take the leg.

'I remember saying, 'Just give me the consent form!', to let me sign it quick. I was still conscious and was still aware of my surroundings, so rather than my mam signing it I said, 'Give it to me.' I signed the form and that was it. I went into theatre, they took above the knee and I spent 12 or 13 days in Waterford Regional recovering.'

This August will mark 18 years since the truck crash which sent Christy McElligott's life on a completely different course. It was immensely traumatic, he says, changing his life in a multitude of ways in terms of his family life, his work as a truck driver, and causing him to turn away from football in almost every capacity; playing, watching, everything, for a number of years.

This was one of the hardest aspects of the struggle, he admits, that sense of his identity tied hand-in-hand with sport being lost. It was who he was. 'Ask anyone,' he says. 'If you asked anybody about Christy McElligott, it was always about football. Christy the footballer. It was difficult and I lost my love of football.

'I didn't want to be around it because I started to see people take advantage of what they had, the opportunities that they had. Those first few years after the accident gave me a lot of time to think about everything, and maybe to overthink it. I started piling on the weight and was starting to get very depressed in how I looked, in my appearance and not wanting to do anything.'

But what defines his journey is an inspirational desire and an internal motivation to not give up. To find a different way to express oneself and not to accept limitations or be defined by them.

Coming face-to-face with death and choosing to, quite literally, fight to preserve his life gave him an entirely new perspective. In the immediate aftermath of the crash, McElligott discovered a new courage and toughness, kicking through the glass of his truck's windshield and clawing to safety with what strength he had left.

'I don't know what happened with me kicking in the window,' he says. 'It was just instinct. I just wanted to get out. I think that's what it was, the adrenaline inside me. I was the fittest I ever was at that time. I was playing with the AUL team, I was playing with the Ireland Junior international team as well, I was playing with Ballymun United and I was also playing Gaelic on a Saturday too.

'I actually did think I was going to die. The funny thing is, it really does take you back and helps you put life into perspective. I was sitting there on the ground in the middle of nowhere and it was so peaceful. There was no pain whatsoever and I could've easily just dozed off, fell asleep and never woke up again. There was no fear, no nothing.

'So, for me, it was really peaceful and really easy for me to do it, if I could [fall asleep]. But again, it was the response of the emergency services to get there as quick as they did and to keep me alive and still awake in the back of the ambulance going from one place to another. I went from Tullow all the way to Limerick and managed to stay awake the whole way there.

'It puts things into perspective. Afterwards I was thinking 'Jesus, the amount of time I gave to football, and was it really that important?' I used to eat, sleep, drink football. I never used to drink and never even smoked. Even when the lads would go out for a few beers after games, I was there sipping blackcurrant.

'I committed everything to football and then it was just gone. Looking back on it, the amount of sacrifices you make and things you give up for football... the rewards are definitely worth it, but when it's gone like that,' he snaps his fingers again. 'You're saying to yourself: 'God, I could've done so much more with the time I had, when I had it.' I think I did feel like I was being robbed of something, definitely.

'But I put it down to the fact that the decision was made for me. I didn't have the opportunity to make that decision, somebody or something else made it for me. I kept saying to myself: 'Just be happy that you're alive.' There was no point in dwelling on what happened, it was important to look forward.'

Fast forward nearly two decades on from the accident and McElligott has completely reinvented himself and has long since found a new lease of life. One of the most decorated amputee footballers in this country, the 49-year-old helped found the Irish Amputee Football Association seven years ago and is now also manager of Ireland's international amputee team.

He has travelled across the world representing Ireland on the international stage, has won league and cup titles, individual awards for his service too. He went to the 2017 Amputee European Championships in Turkey and just a few months ago helped Ireland to 13th place at the 2018 Amputee World Cup which was held in Mexico. He also took part in RTÉ's Operation Transformation two years ago.

More than all of this though, having worked for the last number of years in the FAI's Football For All Programme (firstly as a volunteer and now as a full-time employee helping people with disabilities) the Dubliner has fought to give other amputee footballers a voice, the opportunity and the platform to play at the highest competitive level possible.

Last year saw the first ever season of the Irish Amputee National League take place, with 2019 seeing the competition go from strength-to-strength in its second year. Currently there are three teams competing: Shamrock Rovers, Cork City and Bohemians. The Leesiders were crowned inaugural champions last year and this month travel to Georgia to take part in the first-ever Amputee Champions League.

As coordinator of the league, McElligott says there are plans to see as many as six teams north and south of the border compete, in order to give as many amputee players across the entire country the chance to play football and be recognised as the top-level athletes they are.

Playing five-a-side matches every three weeks, footballers in the Irish Amputee National League play on crutches without prosthetics. The feedback since last year's debut campaign has been overwhelmingly positive, McElligott says. It is an outlet that allows players to discover, or rediscover, a love of football, taking ownership of their experience.

'The players love it,' he smiles. 'The players themselves really enjoy competitive football. But they also enjoy the bond and camaraderie that it creates. We get away with slagging each other off, because we're all amputees.

'We've all gone through similar experiences, so we get away with saying these things to each other. But outside of it, if somebody was to say something to one of us, we'd really flip. We believe that we're taking ownership of who we are.

'We've been lucky to have a great group of players who all want to play football. These players want to be considered as athletes and we don't go into the dressing room and talk about our problems. It's not one of those cases where I want to know what happened to someone else. I want to know if you can play football, that's all that matters.

'We founded the Irish Amputee Football Association seven years ago,' he explains. 'We started the international team first and it came under the umbrella of the FAI's Football For All Programme.

'We had two or three years of training and playing games. We played against Italy, against France, Poland, England. Gradually we started to move up the ladder and then after the Euros in 2017, it was always a decision to set up our own league.

'Now every three weeks Shamrock Rovers, Cork City and Bohemians play at Roadstone, Ballymun and down in Cork too. Each team has about 10 players signed. We've been gifted with a huge amount of arm amputees, who can only be goalkeepers.

'The outfield players have to play on crutches on one leg. We don't play using the prosthetic. In England they do, but we don't, because we see it as a health and safety risk.

'A new team has just started up in Belfast. Down the line, going to plan, they will come in and play in the Irish Amputee League, meaning it could potentially be the first All-Ireland league. There is a possibility of a Limerick side coming in next year, too. If we can get to five or six teams in the next few years, that would be brilliant.

'Unfortunately we don't have a lot of wars in this country,' McElligott jokes, addressing the player pool for amputee football in Ireland. 'We don't have landmines that people are stepping on and stuff like that — unlike in other countries in Europe and across the world.

'Most of the Irish amputee footballers in this country are either born with a congenital defect or have lost it through trauma, like an accident. But all they want to do is play football.'

Currently completing his Uefa A licence, constantly striving to expand the national league, managing the Irish international team and also making time to still compete as a striker for Shamrock Rovers, McElligot's life is busy, but he says he wouldn't have it any other way.

You just don't know where life will take you, he admits. So much of his life has revolved around football and even the day which changed his life forever in August 2001 was brought about because he wanted to play a friendly game for Ballymun.

Then captain, having led the side to the FAI Junior Cup just six weeks beforehand, McElligott didn't want to miss out on a pre-season friendly game and chose to start his truck shift earlier in the morning, so he could make it back in time for the match.

Had he decided to skip the friendly, life would have been very different, he says. But he is resolute that he would not change his experience if given the opportunity. That lorry crash, a horrific and traumatic experience for anyone to go through, has made him the man he is today.

'I wouldn't change it for one second because becoming an amputee has opened so many doors for me,' he states. 'Doors that wouldn't have been an avenue I would have investigated at any other stage have opened for me because of what happened.

'I always put it back to having no regrets. You can always beat yourself up saying: 'Remember that time you didn't take the opportunity to go on trial with Man United', 'Remember that time you didn't have a rest for that friendly game for Ballymun the morning the accident happened', 'Remember that time you...,' he pauses.

'I remember all those situations in my life. For me, it's just about trying to enjoy every minute of time I have. To try and be the best coach I possibly can, to help people understand football, to try and give them the opportunity to play. And hopefully help others get as much enjoyment out of football as I have done and still do to this day.'

THIRTEEN

AFTER THE GARDEN

—

GAVAN CASEY | 4 JUNE

A NIGHT FOR the ages at Madison Square Garden reminded us again that the boxing ring, so often the theatre of the expected, remains an undisputed refuge for magic when two huge men collide at centre-stage.

A fight for the ages between two women of indisputable might copper-fastened the sport's dark side in the minds of many; the wrong woman taking home all the gold, the right woman heading home to her day job as, well, a copper.

It seems strange given the nutty 'lack-of-coverage' debate which preceded it, that Katie Taylor's crowning moment will be a hot-button topic in the Irish media this week, not for the magnitude of her achievement in becoming the country's first undisputed world champion of the modern era, but for the impending debate as to whether or not we should dispute it.

For why should we, the Irish people, perennial sufferers of sporting injustice, not equally wail into the abyss when the shoe is on the other foot?

There will be column inches dedicated to the hypocrisy in our once more lauding Taylor as the greatest Irish person to have ever lived while Delfine Persoon returns to the beat in Belgium minus the WBC belt she held for five years, and minus the four other belts many contend should have sat safely in her overhead locker on the long flight home from New York.

Very few of them actually cover or even follow boxing but the Venn diagram of those who will this week tell us police officer Persoon was the victim of a scandalous heist, and those who have previously written off Taylor's professional pursuit on the basis that some of her opponents have day jobs, will probably be a full circle.

Persoon is within her rights to protest, for sure.

And she intends for her appeal to be heard while not expecting it to be adhered to.

'What we will do now is, of course, make a complaint,' she told the Belgian publication Sudpresse. 'But without much hope because the weight of the Belgian boxing does not weigh heavy in the instances.

'Now, all the better if we manage to move the lines a little in this area. But with my coach we will also quietly analyse this fight sequence by sequence, to have all the arguments to present an unassailable file.

'I said before I left for New York that if I did not win by KO, the judges would never give me the victory, and that's exactly what happened.'

If the shoe had been on the other foot, would Ireland have raged on Taylor's behalf? We would have gone nuclear.

But that doesn't necessarily mean we would have been right; it doesn't necessarily mean Persoon or anyone else is right to believe she had victory snatched from her by some nefarious force.

Be it through sheer incompetence or, on occasion, something shadier, many professional boxing judges now show a borderline comical disregard for doing their jobs properly. The terms 'robbery' and 'corruption' are as a result passed around like an extra bag of chips, the go-to comfort food for those who watched an underdog flip the supposed script on a heavy favourite only to have their fairytale curtailed by the pesky adjudicators.

And because boxing is so sodden with actual robberies, we can begin to build the latest scandal in our heads, or with our thumbs, before it even comes to fruition.

There have been recent fights, like both Gennady Golovkin-Canelo Alvarez middleweight showdowns, where we have turned on our TVs or walked through the turnstiles with a fearful apprehension as opposed to a feverish anticipation. And our foreboding was proven justified — definitely the first time, anyway.

Golovkin was robbed blind that night. It's that type of unabashed bollocksology which rightly drives prospective fans away from the sport.

Persoon was not the victim of some underhanded miscarriage of justice on Saturday night, and to put her battle with Taylor in the same tainted bracket is in itself unjust.

Adding to the West Flanders woman's sense of injustice was the incident which saw her moved to a separate New York hotel after one night spent under the same roof as Taylor; her trainer and partner Filiep Tampere accused Taylor of 'total disrespect' in her demand that he and his fighter find new accommodation. Taylor and her own team denied on separate occasions that she had anything to do with it or even had any knowledge of it.

Her manager Brian Peters put it down to a misunderstanding, describing it as 'industry standard policy' for fighters to stay in separate hotels.

The Belgian camp again cried foul when she had to give extra blood tests hours before the fight at the behest of the New York State Athletic Commission (NYSAC); Persoon has asthma for which she uses an inhaler. She doesn't require a prescription and when used in regulation, the inhaler is not prohibited by the World Anti-Doping Agency (WADA). The doctor in New York, however, reportedly required further proof that Persoon did not have hepatitis B, the reactivation of which can be linked to certain asthma treatments.

Meirhaeghe Maarten, a doctor for Belgian pro cycling team Lotto Soudal who also works with Persoon, described it as 'completely unnecessary', adding: 'Delfine is completely in accordance with the rules of WADA, but apparently they have their own rules here, which are not transparent at all. And for Katie Taylor they are not nearly meticulous as for Delfine — she does not have to take new tests. I can't get rid of the impression that the medical committee plays with the organisation — without talking about a conspiracy, does it?'

Then came what Team Persoon and plenty of onlookers allege to have been the greatest conspiracy of all — what happened in the ring.

Only it wasn't one.

Fights are scored on a round-by-round basis, not on a general hunch or a vibe; not by whoever finishes stronger or is less tired; not by whoever's face holds up the better or by whoever's hair is the least ruffled come final bell.

And the majority of the rounds in Taylor and Persoon's compelling contest were about as close as conceivably possible.

Scoring it from within the arena on Saturday night, I had it a draw at 95-95. Watching it back on Sunday morning, I saw a couple of rounds differently but wound up with the same final tally.

It's only one man's perception of events from two different perspectives, and if you disagree with it, that's absolutely fine. Loads do. Plenty don't.

Here's the thing: you could make a case for Taylor winning at least four of the first five rounds, or you could make a case for her winning only one or two of them. You could make the case for her winning rounds six, eight and nine in the latter half of the fight, or one of them, or two of them, or none of them.

Every round from one to 10 is worth the same and, in all, there were enough contentious rounds there to make the case that Taylor just about did enough, even if most didn't see it that way. I personally had her doing enough only to avoid defeat.

On the flipside, you could argue in Persoon's favour for probably every single round bar the sixth.

The Belgian's was the stronger case for victory. It just wasn't the only case.

Theirs was a great fight but also a grey one, not black and white. It happens.

Persoon wagged her finger and exited the ring understandably distraught whereas Taylor rightly cut a relieved figure. That conspicuous exhalation wasn't some admission of guilt, just a natural and exhausted reaction to her emerging victorious from a gruelling nail-biter.

The verdict evoked guttural cheers which tested the sturdiness of The Garden's roof. There was a sprinkling of boos, too, and not only from the handful of Belgians in the arena.

One of the judges disagreed with the overall verdict reached by the three of them: Don Trella had it 95-95 even. If one of Allen Nace or John Poturaj had seen a single round more for Persoon, they would have had arrived at the same conclusion. The fight would have entered the history books as a draw. That's how close they had it.

'Typical Eddie Hearn,' the sceptics will cry, for the margins at play here are slender to the point that they might seem almost... convenient?

Taylor was, of course, the Hearn fighter, the house fighter, the shining star; the promotional A-side and the marketing upside.

But whatever influence you may allege Hearn or any other promoter to exert over judges, the Englishman's impish charm must have worn thin at Madison Square Garden on Saturday: at the time when one of his other fighters, Tommy Coyle, was stopped by 'away' opponent Chris Algieri earlier in the evening, Coyle was down by three rounds on two cards and seven on the other; in the fight before Taylor's, one of Hearn's most hotly touted prospects, former British Olympian Josh Kelly, was held to a surprising and momentum-killing draw on what was supposed to be his unveiling to America; in the main event, the face of Hearn's entire transatlantic boxing enterprise, Anthony Joshua, was trailing on two of the three cards during his own Stateside bow before 'Mexican Rocky' Andy Ruiz floored him twice more and lowered the curtain in the seventh.

It was probably the most disastrous night of Eddie Hearn's entire career, and bear in mind this is a man whose bare arse was unveiled to the world during an egregious 'pantsing' incident last October.

Katie Taylor simply got a contentious nod, and barely. It could have gone the other way. It could easily have been a draw. In any case, Taylor will be the most disputed undisputed world champion in boxing for the foreseeable future.

Which brings us to a verdict upon which we can all agree: Persoon is more than worthy of a rematch and they simply must do it again.

The WBC, who could feel as though they owe one to their long-reigning former champion, might even wind up mandating a sequel. They commissioned some sort of commemorative pink bracelet for Saturday's victor so God only knows what else they're capable of.

But if they don't demand one, Katie Taylor will.

In her hotel in the early hours of Sunday morning, there was a smile which escaped through the bumps, bruises and stitches — 'We both had to get stitches, I think, from the head clashes,' Taylor would say pointedly when asked about the wound on her forehead — but privately she'll be seething.

With her overall performance partially, but predominantly the fact that she left the door open for a debate at all. (Away from the judging controversy, Persoon will feel similarly aggrieved that she didn't pour it on slightly sooner; another minute at her disposal, and there would likely have been nothing to debate).

Taylor and her team will have questions as to how Persoon — day job and all (albeit with a full camp behind her; she was given extra time by her employers to prepare for the fight) — seemed to have plenty more rounds left in the tank at the death while Taylor herself physically wilted.

The Irishwoman might have made things easier for herself only for her immense sense of pride to work to her detriment. As she acknowledged from behind her five belts back at HQ: 'I probably just stood there with her a bit too much, but that's the way it goes; that's my personality, that's my nature; I do love a good tear-up.'

Her team have 'other plans' on the immediate horizon, which they say won't necessarily change for Persoon, but the festering question mark will doubtless put Taylor on their case to make it happen before long.

If the theme to her professional career has been redemption to this juncture, it's about to take on a vindication story arc which can only be closed off by Taylor and Persoon resuming what became overnight a rivalry fierce and fascinating in equal measure.

Casual interest in her 'road to undisputed' suffered for the fact that the journey became procession-like through no fault of her own. Diehards continued to marvel at Taylor's ring brilliance in the wee hours but plenty became content to wait for a result in the morning, sleeping soundly in the knowledge that they'd wake up to find that Katie Taylor had won again, 'and sure isn't she brilliant'.

Persoon came within a whisker of derailing the entire thing, and in her mighty effort certainly eroded the sense of invincibility and inevitability that Taylor had recultivated in the paid ranks.

Minutes before their captivating contest, Taylor arrived to a noise which blew even her away, U2's I Still Haven't Found

What I'm Looking For bellowed out by the 12,000 or so people who had taken their seats at that point.

It was a memorable moment spoiled only fractionally by the assumption that Taylor herself almost certainly didn't choose the song. She later confirmed as much with a laugh, crediting manager Brian Peters who added with a wry smile: 'We won't have to play that tune again!'

They might. But in a female fight for the ages with Delfine Persoon, Taylor found more than undisputed title success: she met her match, and the impending friction between them could spark a little bit of magic.

'Winning that way — okay, officially she is the winner, but if I would watch the match again in her case I wouldn't want to go on living like that either,' Persoon has said since. 'I'd rather lose it unjustly than win unjustly.'

Chances are, there'll be many more eyes on them when they eventually meet in the middle once more.

FOURTEEN

KEEPER OF THE FAITH

—

PAUL DOLLERY | 31 DECEMBER

IT WAS AN inauspicious start to a season that John Kerins is unlikely to forget. A Tuesday evening back in April, and the players on the Ballinlough pitch outnumbered the spectators who turned up to see St Finbarr's beaten handily by St Michael's in the first round of the Cork City Division Junior A Football Championship.

With an 11-point loss for his club's third-string team in his first championship outing of 2018, Kerins couldn't have been much further away from the dream scenario he found himself in when the year drew to a close. That the 26-year-old goalkeeper is now the owner of a senior county medal is a fact he's still attempting to process.

A first Cork senior football championship title in 33 years for one of the county's most illustrious clubs provided a captivating narrative in itself. John Kerins' role added another fascinating angle to the tale of how the men from Togher ended a long wait for that elusive triumph.

'At the start of the year I was probably third or fourth in the choice of goalkeepers in the club,' says Kerins. 'I remember we got a bit of a trimming from St Michael's with the juniors. It definitely wasn't the most encouraging start to the year. But circumstances ultimately dictated that I ended up having a bit of a crazy rise.'

Going into the 2017 final against Nemo Rangers, St Finbarr's had eight Cork senior football titles — as well as three All-Irelands — to their name. However, succumbing to their southside city neighbours after a replay meant that the Barrs had fallen short in each of their last eight appearances on county final day.

That run of misfortune extended back to their defeat to Imokilly in 1986, when Kerins' father — John Senior — was the goalkeeper on a Blues team bidding to retain the Andy Scannell Cup, which they won at Clonakilty's expense the previous year.

For goalkeepers, patience is a vital virtue in the pursuit of an opportunity to make an impression. John Kerins Junior has had plenty of it for the best part of a decade.

He won two county medals at minor level, restricted to a back-up role in both victories. On the senior panel that was beaten by Nemo in last year's final, he trailed both Declan Murphy and James McDonnell in the goalkeeping pecking order.

'As a goalkeeper, something has to happen for you to get into the team,' Kerins explains. 'It's generally a matter of circumstance. You're just hoping and hoping that things will eventually fall in your favour.

'I remember being in the gym two weeks after the county final last year. I was doing three days a week and we were back on the field then at the start of January. Maybe fitness isn't seen as being as important for goalkeepers as it is for the other lads, but I wanted to show that I was putting the work in.

'But was I thinking about being the senior goalkeeper in a county final at that stage? Absolutely not,' he laughs. 'A million miles from it. My focus was probably on pushing James [McDonnell] to be second-choice instead of carrying water.

'As the year went on, things sort of worked out well for me. I can't really claim it was down to form. James had to step away for a couple of months because of work and family commitments, so I played two championship games for the intermediates — the third round and the quarter-final.'

By the time they took on Aghabullogue in the semi-final of the Cork intermediate football championship on 13 October, the Barrs' second-string side were forced to change their goalkeeper once more. Three weeks earlier, Kerins had been thrown into the deep end.

With just over 10 minutes of the senior quarter-final against Douglas remaining, Declan Murphy was stretchered off with a broken leg. Kerins was sprung from the bench for his first taste of the top grade, completing the rare treble of playing junior, intermediate and senior championship football for one club in the same season.

'In all honesty, I was absolute bricking it when I came on,' he admits. 'I was more nervous for those few minutes than I was for the county final. Self-doubt creeps in massively.

"Am I able for this?' — that sort of thing.

'We went down to 14 men as well so Douglas were dominant. In the back of your mind is the thought that this is going to go wrong and you're going to be the scapegoat. If me coming on changed that game for Douglas, I'd never be seen again. Good luck!

'Our backs were to the wall, but thankfully we got out of it. Coming through it was huge for me in terms of the mental strength it brought. The semi-final and the final afterwards were a breeze in comparison.'

A 0-15 to 0-12 win over Carbery provided the Barrs with another opportunity to banish their county final hoodoo. That 33-year wait finally ended at Páirc Uí Chaoimh on the last weekend in October, as they came out on the right side of a 3-14 to 2-14 scoreline following a thrilling encounter with Duhallow.

Two victories separated by more than three decades, yet inextricably linked by the goalkeeper on each occasion. As was the case in 1985 when the Barrs last reached the summit of Cork football, the number one jersey in 2018 was worn by John Kerins.

'The funny thing is that if my dad was still around he'd probably have me playing out the field instead of in goal,' John Jr. says of his two-time All-Star father, a legendary figure in Cork GAA, having won six Munster senior titles and two All-Irelands with the Rebels.

In August 2001, three months after being diagnosed with cancer, he passed away at 39, survived by his wife Anne and children Suzanne, Paul and John, who was the eldest of the three children at just nine years of age. A substantial presence from Meath at the funeral revealed to him the esteem in which his father was held.

'To me at that stage he was just my dad. I can still remember being about four years old and going out on the green in our estate with my brother Paul [also a member of the current St

Finbarr's panel]. We used to have my dad's jerseys and shorts hanging off us, just kicking a ball around.

'We had all his matches taped so a regular Saturday morning for us would have been getting up out of bed and throwing a video in to watch a couple of his games. We'd have our own little All-Ireland then in the front room. But he was still just dad to us. We didn't see him as someone who was well-known or anything.'

John Kerins was the goalkeeper on the Cork team that developed a bitter rivalry with Meath in the late 1980s. The Royals were victorious in back-to-back All-Ireland finals in '87 and '88. A 16-year wait for Sam Maguire ended when the Rebels beat Mayo in the '89 final, before they finally exacted sweet revenge over Meath in the 1990 decider.

'After my dad passed away, fellas would often come up and tell me stories about him. It kind of sunk in then how much he was respected. All the Meath lads turning up to the funeral was a big part of that.

'I would have heard plenty about how much bad blood there was between the teams. They actually ended up in the same resort on holiday one year and they wouldn't speak a word to each other. They couldn't even be in the same room. That's how much tension was there.

'Things are much different now. There's a great relationship between our family and the Meath lads. The funeral just seemed to lift all the tension. After the county final I got lovely messages from fellas on that team like Gerry McEntee and Robbie O'Malley.

'Any time we're in Dublin, Robbie will come down from Meath just to meet for a cup of coffee or a bite to eat. There's a huge amount of respect there. Again, that's the kind of thing that hits home about my dad and makes me realise how highly people thought of him.'

The presence of the son of the late John Kerins between the posts for the Barrs added significantly to this year's emotionally charged county final victory. Also at the forefront of the players' minds was Kevin McTernan, the club's goalkeeper in the 2009 and '10 finals, who too would have savoured the occasion. After a long illness, he died on the eve of the replay defeat to Nemo Rangers in last year's final.

'The day before the county final this year I was up at my dad's grave. The morning of the game I was at Kevin McTernan's,' says Kerins. 'Going to my dad's grave was probably a nervous tension thing as much as anything else. I wouldn't class myself as a spiritual person at all, but I just asked him to keep me settled, keep me cool.

'When the game had gone beyond the 60 minutes and we were ahead, I turned and looked at the scoreboard. I looked up to the heavens then and just said 'Get us through this, please!'

'When the whistle went, it was just pandemonium. It was just an unreal thing to be a part of with your club. It's hard to put into words what that club means personally.

'It's been a lot more to me during my life than an outlet for sport. It's everything. To see the elation on the faces of so many people, nothing could top it.

'On the pitch afterwards, someone said to me that my mam was around, which caught me off guard as she didn't actually go to the game because of the nerves. But it turned out that she had decided to go in for the last 10 minutes. As soon as I saw her, that was me done.

'Seeing her emotion after the game, you just knew right away that it was something special. My sister ran onto the pitch as well, she was one of the first people to hug me. My cousin was with her and I wouldn't say he'd be the type to cry often, but he was in tears.

'My brother Paul was the same. Just to see what it meant to my family, you're reminded that it's more than just a game. Everything comes back to family. That's what keeps me going. It was a fairly special day, one that will stick with me for a long time.'

After enduring such a long drought, St Finbarr's will be eager to retain their status as Cork champions beyond 2019.

For now, John Kerins is savouring some down-time. At the top of his agenda for the festive period is another visit to St Catherine's cemetery in Kilcully.

His father has waited long enough to be reunited with the Andy Scannell Cup.

FIFTEEN

LIVING THE DREAM, SURVIVING THE PAIN

—

DAVID SNEYD | 25 MAY

ALAN MOORE USED to love writing stories in school.

For a little while they would be about horses and ponies and the trips he would take with his father and younger brother from their home in south Finglas to the tracks in Portmarnock or Coolock.

His father had horses in a stable by the airport, he would spend his early mornings taking care of them before going to work for Dublin Corporation. At weekends things would get really serious. 'The American Harness Racing, with the chariots, that's what they would race,' Moore recalls.

Slowly, his interest waned. 'I had to get away from them. It wasn't for me at all. I fell off, I was kicked, all sorts. Even now I don't like horses. They're just too powerful for me.'

Just one of the many vulnerabilities he is willing to reveal over the course of a weekend in which the 44-year-old reflects on his life to this point.

Moore was 11 when he left his father and brother to the

horses. By that stage, Rivermount Boys Football Club was the centre of his universe. Based within the deep Tolka Valley, it is a place that looks as if it would close in and swallow you up with one bad touch.

For Alan Moore it opened his mind to the exciting possibilities of a different future.

It was the start of a dream.

The stories he wrote changed.

As he prepared for his Inter Cert (Junior Cert in new money), he continued to dream on the pages of his copybook at Patrician College — 'the football school' — to the point a letter was sent to the family home urging him, well, to cop on and concentrate on getting a proper job.

'That was the school Ronnie Whelan went to. I knew it could be done. In my head I was looking at playing for Ireland in the 1994 World Cup. I worked it out that I would be old enough by then and it was achievable.'

Others knew it was, too.

'Alan was such a graceful player,' Joe Bennett, one of the founding members of Rivermount, beams. Joe is in his 70s now and only recently finished the latest bout of chemotherapy. Speaking about 'young Alan' only brings joy. 'He would be there one second and gone the next, gone by his man before he knew it. He was so shy compared to the others.'

'He always made things look so easy,' Pat Fenlon, another of the Rivermount graduates who later managed him at Shelbourne, recalls. 'He was so smart, he had a football brain. He was quiet, determined, but did things on a pitch that would excite you.'

Alan Moore enjoyed and endured 10 years at Middlesbrough at a time when the club went on a feckless, cash-mad spree through the Premier League. He earned eight senior caps for Ireland — captaining all the underage sides along the way — and played for Barnsley, Burnley, Shelbourne, Sligo Rovers and Derry City, before calling it quits at the age of 33.

He scored one of the most important — almost forgotten — goals for a League of Ireland club in Europe, when he struck late away to Hajduk Split for Shels to nab the second away goal which proved crucial in helping to set up that famous Champions League clash with Deportivo La Coruna.

'It fucking annoys me that people don't remember,' Stephen McGuinness, a childhood friend who is now general secretary of the PFA Ireland, says.

'It's not like Skip [McGuinness] to get angry,' Moore chuckles.

There has been one divorce, followed by a second marriage to the wonderful, inspiring, caring Lucie that has given them three beautiful daughters — Sadie (15), Lexie (13) and Brontie (seven).

So, the day his career finished was not a sad day. He was ready for it, even if it was forced by another back injury.

This was the day he believed the pain would finally stop, that he wouldn't have to take another pill and could actually dare to hold one of his daughters for longer than a few moments before the agony became too much.

'I wanted to have a normal life with Lucie and the kids, but it doesn't actually fucking work out that way. It doesn't work out that way. I still need pills.'

For the slipped disc and nerve damage that required back surgery.

For both his knees that were operated on.

For the calves with improper blood flow that meant he had to learn to walk again not long after celebrating his 21st birthday.

For the Achilles that he snapped.

The pain was only beginning.

His back got worse.

His knees got worse.

His legs got worse.

His Achilles got worse.

'My whole fucking body keeled in,' Moore sighs.

Rebound headaches started soon after he binned the tablets, painful migraines that continue to this day, engulfing his mind in a cloud because of his dependency on medication. He is back on painkillers, as proven by opening up the cubbyhole between the driver and passenger seat in his car.

'My little pharmacy,' he deadpans. 'I can't pass a super-market without picking up paracetamol or ibuprofen because I can't risk running out.'

There were countless epidurals to stave off back surgery, before it was a necessity. So many injections to get through games it would be impossible to count. Some of the medication he counts off hand to help relieve pain include Voltarol (causes havoc with the stomach), Brufen, Gabapentin (an antidepressant prescribed after his back surgery) and Difene, the anti-inflammatory which only last year was linked to an increased risk of heart attack and stroke by the British Medical Journal.

The physical damage has been a blight since his early 20s. He is by no means immune but there is almost a numbness after what he has put his body through. There are times in conversation when you are met by a glaze and wonder if things are being taken in.

But they are.

'I've always been comfortable in my own skin,' he adds.

And yet, there was a time he wasn't.

That physical anguish is easy to deal with compared to his mental health. Suicidal thoughts which first took hold during his teens manifested itself in the summer prior to his 40th birthday in November 2014.

He tried to take his own life.

Twice.

Two overdoses.

Both times Lucie was there to prevent the worst and now, five years on, he is no longer in complete darkness. But there are still questions.

'You want to know why you feel like this. You want to know, 'Why I am like this?' You want to know what has changed and made you get into this fucking situation where you want to kill yourself.'

Those questions have not yet been answered.

But the one for this story is this: has it all been worth it?

* * *

The 2pm train from Leeds to Skipton arrives bang on 2.40pm and Moore is waiting outside. The sun is beaming, it's still early and the weekend awaits enticingly. This will be a busy end to an already hectic week in what has been an arduous season.

The Dubliner now works as an opposition analyst for Wigan Athletic, where Paul Cook, his former Burnley teammate, and later Sligo manager, is in charge. It is Friday, 12 April and the Latics are in a relegation dogfight in the Championship.

They are level on 41 points with Millwall and Reading — two points clear of Rotherham United in the drop zone. Ipswich Town and Bolton Wanderers are already down. The season is coming to a nail-biting conclusion and the first of five cup finals is on Sunday.

Wigan host leaders, the champions-elect, Norwich City. Moore arrived back to Lancashire from Norfolk on Thursday after an eight-hour, 400-mile round trip to watch their 2-2 draw with Reading at Carrow Road on Wednesday night.

Tomorrow morning there will be one final, early-morning briefing at Wigan's training ground before taking in the U18 academy game between Blackburn Rovers and Wolverhampton Wanderers 20 miles away at midday.

After that it will be across the Pennines to Elland Road for Leeds United's Yorkshire derby with Sheffield Wednesday, the aim being to provide hope for Cook as he looks to outwit Marcelo Bielsa in Wigan's bid for survival.

But before all that, we're heading to the pub.

'Lucie and the girls have gone ice-skating,' Moore explains, as we set off on the 15-minute journey towards the small, picturesque village of Gisburn where they live. It is enveloped by hills and a sense of calm.

'A few pints then back to the house for dinner later on.'

This is certainly the day for it.

Moore speaks with a disarming softness, almost a groggy drawl. There is nothing bombastic or brash. He seems slightly on edge, though, perhaps because I am not the only visitor this weekend.

Sadie, his eldest, has her boyfriend Josh staying too. He plays in the same Middlesbrough youth side as Callum Kavanagh, son of former Boro and Ireland teammate Graham, who just happens to be one of his best friends.

Moore knows footballers inside out and sees only good in this one. 'He has a kind soul, I think. He seems a nice kid and wants to do things the right way. And I told him I'd kneecap him if he messed her about.'

The tone never changes. You don't know if he means it or not.

'Well, he doesn't know if I do so that's the main thing.'

He doesn't mean it, but no harm keeping Josh on edge. Indeed, the two will go to the Wigan-Norwich game together on Sunday afternoon.

The Aspinall Arms in the heart of the Ribble Valley in nearby Clitheroe is our first port of call. Sitting in a conservatory looking out at the river flow by, this is the sort of English pub where it seems safe to order a pint of Guinness.

Moore has been kind enough to welcome me into his world, one he has always been happy to keep closed off from those he is unsure of. 'That's always been mistaken as arrogance but it's just me. We are all different. I was a footballer and people expect something different of you. I never sought fame or money or anything else. I just loved playing football and was happy to be away in the countryside as soon as the match was over.'

This place is heaven. And so is the Guinness. Moore, after dallying over his order, is sticking with Peroni. 'I don't know what I want anymore.'

We sit and chat and start at the beginning. The horses and ponies never stood a chance once football came on the scene.

He had a paper round earning £2.50 a week, all of which went towards a £40 pair of Puma Kings.

He was in love, but Finglas in the 1980s was not the sort of place where that was enough.

'There was great hardship for my parents. I was going on all these trials over to England and I knew they had to put their hands in their pocket for me. The money wasn't always there. We had to fight for everything. Everything. They never came to see me play so there was never any pressure on me, I had no one shouting and screaming on the line so that helped and they let me choose whichever club I wanted to.'

He was 12 when Jack Charlton became manager of the Republic of Ireland and in his early teens when Ray Houghton put the ball in the English net. Moore learned to play on the street, the family Alsatian, Buster, helping sharpen his dribbling skills when weary friends had enough. 'The dog would bite at my ankles. It taught me to move fast fucking quickly,' he laughs.

And he did, eventually signing for Middlesbrough at 16 when bigger clubs also chased his signature.

He didn't like that Manchester United brought him over for several trials and placed him in the Salford University halls of residence with 30 other hopefuls. 'I am shy, an introvert, imagine what that's like when you're a kid?' he reasons.

At Chelsea and Queens Park Rangers he could hardly hear himself think because of the busy Heathrow flight path above. Then it looked as if his story had the twist he craved. Liverpool, the club he supported, offered him a two-year scholarship.

Moore rejected it.

'In my own mind I knew my worth and what I wanted,'

he says. 'I knew I could hold out for a professional contract somewhere else.'

Evidence that shyness should not be mistaken for weakness.

Our pints are now foamy stains on the glass. It's my shout. 'Guinness and Peroni, please, mate,' my Dublin accent slowing to avoid having to repeat the order.

'How much for cash?' I joke. They are only going to get worse as the day goes on.

Moore is gone when I return. As the minutes go by and his absence lingers I begin to wonder... this wouldn't be such a bad place to be left stranded. The flow of the river outside is mesmeric. The Guinness even more so.

Moore returns, explaining a friend was around the corner, and we continue, his answers delivered in that disarming Dublin drawl that is somewhat diminished, but not completely, after almost 30 years away.

'There are no football pictures in the house, I have my Ireland caps in a box somewhere, my Ma has some things framed in the house but they're not on the walls or on display,' he admits.

His girls may not have their father's previous life rubbed in their faces but they have the football bug. 'If they need help of course I'll help. Maybe I could get them an Alsatian like I had. I'll get out the back with cones and do what any father would do, spend time with their kids doing what they enjoy. Any child would love that, getting attention from their father and it's not just football, the girls have tried netball too.'

A series of injuries decimated a career which seemed destined for the greatest heights, having played an integral role in Middlesbrough's promotion to the Premier League as First Division champions in 1995.

There is no anger or bitterness, but the hurt is palpable.

'You realise later on they [clubs] don't give a fuck. It's a mentality, you're in a team game, it wasn't about individuals. Now it is. Lads won't play unless they're 100% fit. We had a smaller group, you wanted to be part of it and help. But that began to change when I was playing too.'

* * *

We quickly move on, in the direction of home, but the destination is the impressive Holmes Mill beer hall, where the 5pm crowd is drawing ever closer and a wedding party are in great spirits in the function room to the left of the imposing 105ft bar which splits the room.

'I enjoyed making people happy and entertaining them because that's what football is about,' Moore begins, as we take our seats away from the madness.

'I wanted to make Maradona runs as a kid and make a show of full backs but as you get older you realise you've got to be more productive and make the most of having the ball. But I always wanted to put a smile on people's faces.'

His time at Middlesbrough straddled two different worlds: no money and new money.

From the historical Ayresome Park to the flash new Riverside Stadium, Moore was even used in the publicity shots to mark this brave new world as one of the academy graduates who was destined for stardom.

Lenny Lawrence, the man who gave him his debut, was replaced by the legendary figure of Bryan Robson. The money was rolling in and going out just as quick.

Neil Cox was signed for £1 million — a club record — and the spending continued, £50m in a period of four years.

Brazilian footballer of the year Juninho arrived for £4.75m in October 1995.

Nick Barmby cost more than that again when he joined for £5.25m soon after.

World Cup winner Branco came, so too Emerson, a third Brazilian, for £4m from Porto.

But the one that really put Boro on the map was the £7m capture of Italian superstar Fabrizio Ravanelli, who joined just a couple of months after he scored for Juventus in the 1996 European Cup final.

'It became like a runaway train,' Moore recalls. 'I was lucky that I could step up the levels. I never felt intimidated by the likes of Ravanelli, I just wanted the ball and was like 'Yeah, I'm able for this'.'

Those arrivals caused a stir, more so in their own dressing room than anywhere else. With the average weekly wage previously in the region of between £4,000-6,000, Ravanelli was taking home £42,000 a week.

'A horrible man, a horrible man. He got away with it because he was allowed to. He came into the changing room and would sit with his four Italian agents, he wouldn't speak a word of English to anyone else.

'For away games, he brought his own chef, we'd be in a five-star hotel by the way, but his own chef would cook his pasta because their pasta wasn't good enough. When he got injured he was on the first flight back to Italy all the time. He didn't try a leg away from home when it didn't suit. The stuff he did and got away with was scandalous and that did bring friction, it did bring a divide. I have no problem with players earning big money, you get what you deserve, but Ravanelli was a mercenary.'

This is the first hint of bitterness, of a release that has been building up. It's taken him more than 20 years. For Neil Cox the point of no return came much sooner — on the morning of the 1997 FA Cup final with Chelsea.

'He knocked him out,' Moore laughs. Ravanelli had damaged a hamstring a couple of weeks previously and disappeared to his home country for treatment, arriving back the day before the showpiece to declare himself fully fit.

Cox had already given an interview which then appeared on matchday saying Ravanelli shouldn't play, and the pair came to blows. 'It wasn't mental or some sort of free-for-all, he was just knocked out because Neil had enough. Ravanelli was hated.

'This all hurt me because Middlesbrough is where I became a man, they stood by me with a four-year contract when I was out injured and I got to live out my dreams.'

Moore missed that FA Cup final after damaging his ankle in the semi-final replay, another source of great upset, and he was out for the entirety of the following season as his calf and knee problems wreaked havoc.

By the time he was fit again, Ravanelli, Juninho, Branco and Emerson were long gone. In their place came Paul Merson and Paul Gascoigne.

The madness continued.

A breathalyser was introduced at the training ground for Gazza, an examination he rarely passed. Merson, signed from Arsenal and who would depart in acrimonious circumstances for Aston Villa after just one season, never seemed fully committed.

He was allowed live hundreds of miles away in the south and would commute on the train. Within the first week it became clear he was never going to make it in on time, so the fines' committee — a trio of senior players — made it be known he would have to pay £50 for every minute he would be late.

Not a problem when you're earning over £20,000 a week. 'He came in the next day with cheque for 26 grand. He said he worked it out on the train home that for the days he'll be coming in that would be the amount he would have to pay in fines for the season.'

Still, Moore can appreciate the ability. 'An exceptional player. Miles better than Juninho for me. Not even close. He could do everything on one touch, and he could be good craic. He killed me in training one day.

"What have you got?'

"What do you mean?'

"Well I've got the best outside right foot in the world, so what have you got?'

'That killed me. I'm not competing with that,' Moore laughs.

Boro still managed to make it to three domestic Cup finals — the FA Cup and two League Cups — in '97 and '98. However, they also suffered relegation after being docked points for postponing a fixture due to an outbreak of illness at the club.

'Things were already bleak. The fans loved Juninho and he did some great things but a lot of the problems those lads caused absolutely killed us,' Moore feels.

Gascoigne, unsurprisingly, almost did it for real when he commandeered the team bus before travelling to their first away game of the 1998/99 season with Villa. With an hour to kill in Darlington before departing, the bus was left unattended.

That was enough.

'Gazza set off in it, he flew over speed bumps, some of us were following in a car, he got to the very end of this road with two massive pillars and he has crumpled into it.'

But he's not done…

'He tried to reverse out, he got to the other side of the road and there was this little old lady at a bus stop. He jumped out, threw the keys to the lady and said, 'There's your bus'. He then had to ring the gaffer [Robson] to explain how there had been an accident. There were thousands of pounds worth of damage.'

Plenty would soon be inflicted on Moore, as the writing was on the wall for his career at the top level.

Before getting into that, another couple of pints in another pub. Darkness is still a bit off and his local, The White Bull, is just the place to stay to allow it fall before going home.

* * *

More Guinness and Peroni. More stories and memories.

He played four times for Middlesbrough between the start of the 97/98 season and when his contract ended in 2001. Five appearances on loan at Barnsley barely helped the situation.

'Those years dragged by, they take their toll,' he says.

When both of his calves would sporadically seize up and go solid due to a lack of blood flow, his feet would go numb. 'I had dye injected into my veins to see if there was a blockage. They cut open behind both knees to relieve the build up, I needed 80 stitches in each leg and because the artery was wrapped around the muscle it meant I had to learn to walk again.

'But you can't look back with regrets. Things happen for a reason, some were taken out of my hands but if you keep dwelling on that you will only feel anger, that's not what I want.'

The issue with his calves led to far more problems. 'I had my knee done. I had my Achilles done. The patella tendon in the knee too.'

This is where the advice and treatment he received can be described, at best, as questionable.

'There was bone digging into the patella tendon so they had to cut into that tendon to get through to the bone in the middle. I was told I would be back training in 10 days and playing in two weeks. I went for a 20-minute run with Gary Pallister and I was literally in tears, I said to him that I was sure the surgeon left the blade in there.

'I was given heat patches but was still in agony so went to see someone else about it. Because it was an operation on a tendon I was told it should have been a minimum of six-month recovery, but I was back running after 10 days, so by the time that was all sorted it was another season gone.'

They were quickly disappearing, as his Ireland dreams also disintegrated after making his debut under new boss Mick McCarthy away to the Czech Republic in April 1996. All eight of his international appearances came in the space of seven months that year, from the friendly in Prague, to the US Cup in the States to the three World Cup qualifiers he was involved in, the last of which was a 0-0 draw with Iceland in Dublin.

'Playing for Ireland was the pinnacle of everything I did. Playing at Lansdowne Road, it was unbelievable, it was different to every other football environment I played in because there were so many people there who knew you.

'Everyone was wishing you well and wanted you to do well. The faces you knew. There was no badness. It was a good place to be and it was surreal to play, it was something that I always dreamed of doing. I always felt full of life going home to play for Ireland. It was a distraction from everything else and always gave me such a lift, it was something I wish I didn't want to let go.'

He had no choice. It was taken from him more than anything as his body failed him.

Dinner is ready and we are on the way. A busy home awaits.

* * *

Lucie Moore is born and bred in Burnley, but she is an Irish mammy at heart. When we arrive, the kitchen is warm and full of life.

There is Sadie, Lexie and Brontie, with next door neighbour Harriet adding an extra voice.

Gizmo is the shih tzu, the three cats are Tinkerbell, Buzz and Cinders.

Josh is the boyfriend. There is more meat on a butcher's apron but Alan's initial impression that he is a 'kind soul' seems true as we watch him happily kick a ball around on the tiles with Brontie (or B as the family call her).

B then dribbles the ball up to her father, says hello and sticks it through his legs.

Emmerdale is finishing up and Coronation Street is about to begin in the kitchen. Leicester City v Newcastle is on in the living room, which is separated by a lovely dining room with an impressive brick-work fireplace.

We head in and B follows. Gizmo is never far behind.

'Daddy, what skill did you teach me?' B asks.

'A step over, B,' her dad replies. 'Then the check back and run with the ball. That's all I want you to do, run with the ball close to you.'

'Daddy, where were you born?' B continues.

'In a hospital,' Alan smiles.

'But where?'

'A hospital,' he repeats.

'Where were you born?' he asks.

'In Burnley!' B exclaims proudly.

'And what about Lexie?'

'Oh, oh.'

She's temporarily stumped.

'Lexie was born in Ireland,' she declares.

'That's right, but whereabouts in Ireland?'

'Oh... if I get it right will you throw the ball to me?'

'Of course'

'She was born in a hospital!'

Their laughs fill the room and B's control isn't too bad when the ball does come her way.

Lucie joins the fun with instructions disguised as questions.

'Will you have some lasagne, Dave?'

'Chips?'

'Garlic bread?'

'Another beer?'

B is still on a mission. 'Mummy, where were Lexie and Sadie born?'

'Sadie was born in Chorley, Lexie was born in Drogheda and you were born in Burnley. Everyone was born in different places. Welcome to the world of your father's job.'

The food is devoured. The beers — Corona and Budweiser — are cold and don't last long either. The ice-skating trip earlier in the day is a topic of conversation when Lexie ventures from the kitchen.

'Mum told me you were horrendous,' Alan teases.

'Well I was better than Sadie. Sadie was absolutely useless and wouldn't even go into the middle. How was work, Dad?'

'It was grand. Lexie, tell Dave who is likely to come into his bed later on.'

'A few people. No, not people. Animals! All the cats will come in at some stage throughout the night,' she warns.

Lucie returns.

'Any more food?

'Garlic bread?'

'Chips?'

'We have loads.'

A breather is needed, and as we sit and watch the rest of the football, followed by Gogglebox and one of those panel shows that acts as background noise, the girls (and Josh) make their way upstairs to watch a film.

'We are removing ourselves from the downstairs area,' Sadie announces for comedic effect. 'Goodnight all.'

Alan and Lucie fell in love not long after he signed for Burnley in 2001. He was already married at the time but living a separate life. His first wife remained in Middlesbrough while he lived in a hotel for eight months.

'It was one of the toughest things I had to do, psychologically, the girl done nothing wrong. I just met Lucie and had a different connection, it was powerful. When someone says there is one person out there for everybody I know what they mean, that's what we have.

'It's why I gave her everything in the divorce. It came down to morals to do the right thing. It was lucky that we didn't have kids.'

He started his family with Lucie. They spent the start of their lives together in Burnley before moving to Ireland and buying a house in Navan. Alan's career took him to Shels, Sligo and Derry, and it looked like it would continue in coaching with Shamrock Rovers until Lucie's father died suddenly of a brain haemorrhage.

'We had to move back home,' Moore explains. 'It was just the right thing to do, the only thing. We wrote off a lot of money on the house but it had to be done.'

'I had to come home,' Lucie explains. 'That was such a tough time, you never really recover fully, grief like that stays with you but it's funny, I look at B and see a lot of my dad in her.'

Friday nights are much different for Lucie now. 'When you were playing in Ireland I would have the split screen up watching Emmerdale and checking Teletext for the scores so I knew what to prepare for,' she says, sitting beside Alan on the couch.

'If they got beat or played shit, you weren't having a conversation for three days. You didn't go mad on the beer, you just sulked for days. You needed to have your space and I think part of the problem was you replayed everything in your head about everything that had gone wrong, not just your own game, you worried about the whole team.'

The conversation goes in all different tangents, there are more drinks, laughs and stories. Before we realise it's almost 2am and we have to be up again in a few hours to make it in to Wigan's training ground before eight.

After a brief standoff with Buzz on the bed, my head is finally able to touch the pillow. But not for long.

Morning soon arrives.

* * *

It's just after 6.30am and I'm sticking my head out the window of my room — a view which sees the hills roll towards this lovely farmyard estate — to help sharpen the senses.

A shower helps — a choice of towels had been laid out by Lucie the previous night — and she is in the kitchen smiling before anyone else in the house has stirred.

'Al won't be down until a minute before you have to leave, trust me,' she insists.

I do.

'So then. Coffee? Tea?'

'Coffee, please.'

The fog is beginning to evaporate with every sip — in my head and outside. 'How has he been with you so far?' she asks.

'Has he spoken about depression? He will be open, he will talk,' she continues. 'He's got through it. We had three or four years where it was shit. It was really bad and he tried to take his own life. You could see a demise...

'Ah, he's alive!' Lucie exclaims as Alan enters the kitchen.

We're ready to head for the Wigan training ground around 40 minutes away and just as we are ready to set off Lucie comes out to the drive to point to the window.

B has come to wave her Daddy off.

We sit in silence for a few minutes before I bring up how he dealt with depression after finishing up.

'Stuff like that just creeps up on you. I've been for chats with the PFA and it seems, from what I can gather, that it's something I've had from a young age and is in-built in me. From a young age I had a mindset, which probably sums up where I am with football, I never got too high but did get low.

'I never expected a lot and if anything came above that it was a bonus. That's the same with life, I never expected anything good in life.'

That seems at odds with the teenager who was prepared to turn down Liverpool's scholarship offers and wait for a professional contract elsewhere.

'The glass was always half empty and anything above that was a bonus,' Moore continues. 'Now I am living in constant pain, it wears you down. I used to enjoy golf. I have four sets of clubs in the garage but can't use them. Eventually the pain you're in, even getting up every day, little movements every day, it wears you down every little bit.

'From the age of 20 it was just painkillers. To get out of bed in the morning, my knee, my back, my Achilles; it was a can of Red Bull and painkillers to get into work.

'The ops on both my legs, each leg op took between six and seven hours. To put that into context, a heart bypass takes four-and-a-half hours. So it's a relief when you don't have to play.'

He did his Uefa A coaching licence through the FAI and got a job running Bury's youth set-up before doing the same at Carlisle United.

'I wanted to look after them as human beings as much as footballers. They are kids out of school, thrown into the big bad world, they're now going to work every morning. You want to look after these people and make them good people. You want to give them the best experience you can for those years they're with you, you want to make sure they are alright after football.'

We have only scratched the surface on this topic by the time we've pulled into Wigan's training ground just before 8am. Manager Paul Cook arrives at the same time and it is his booming Scouse accent that is the dominant voice as he invites us into the office he shares with his staff to start the video analysis of how to set up at home to Norwich.

The plasma television screen is linked to a laptop which prepares different scenarios.

Darron Gibson is one of the first of the playing staff to arrive, dropping his head in the office to say good morning.

Goalkeeper coach Nicky Colgan, the former Ireland international, arrives soon after, midway through the presentation, and then, at 8.55am, there is a knock on the back door.

'Reidy!' Cook and his assistant, Leam Richardson, say in unison.

'Always at this time, without fail,' first team coach Anthony Barry, another Scouser, adds.

True enough, Peter Reid, now 62 and on the staff in an advisory capacity, arrives in his full training kit. He pulls up a seat and leans back with his feet on the table beside the couch which myself, Moore and Richardson are squeezed onto.

'So, then, who have we got tomorrow,' Reid jokes.

Cook continues to dictate his plans to the video analyst operating the laptop beneath the massive screen.

They are also devising ways of making the players believe they can get a result before the team meeting at 9am. That is when Moore and I head to the canteen for breakfast.

Salmon and scrambled eggs.

We find a quiet corner and continue the chat. The jokes and laughter which peppered the past hour soon dissipate as he explains what brought on the depression which eventually led to him trying to take his own life.

Taking Lucie's advice, now was the time to get straight to the point.

What led to you trying to take your own life?

'It's hard to put my finger on it. It just sort of creeped up. Lucie will probably say I had depression for fucking years but to get to that stage, it did sort of creep up. It came out of nowhere. There was no one trigger for it.

'Every day, they were the sort of recurring things that would come into my mind.'

That's scary.

'I know. And there was no trigger for it. Whatever build up or what it was. I'd never miss a day's work, but those thoughts would always be there with you. Nobody knows here. Nobody knows here.'

Has that been a risk, to tell people?

'I felt that I got to a stage where I was getting over it when I was at Carlisle and was alright so went to the club to say 'I just want to let you know, I've had a couple of incidents recently. I've tried to take my own life.' The first thing they asked was whether it was stress at work. I said, 'No, it's nothing to do with that, I just said I felt obliged to tell you and I'm ready to crack on with work."

What happened after you took them?

'Lucie came down stairs. She always got up early. I was on the floor in the lounge with tablets around me. She was upset, she was angry telling me what if the kids had come down and found me. But you're not even thinking of them at that stage. I've been for counselling and all the rest of it. It's a waste of fucking time [for me], they don't give you answers. You go in there hoping for answers and they don't give you answers. They just want to listen to you and don't give you any help at all.'

What answers are you looking for?

'You go in and you want to know why you feel like this. You want to know why I am like this. You want to know what has changed and made you get into this fucking situation where you want to kill yourself. So, they go back over your old past and there are little things that crop up. I remember sitting in the Airport Hotel after playing for the Ireland 21s. My ma was there and a couple of the lads having a few drinks and all the rest of it.

'I remember, I always had this thing in my head and I said it to them there, 'Won't live until I'm 23'. I always had this thing where I had a vision of myself driving my car straight into a wall. I was 18 or 19 at the time. I just had it that I won't live past 23. So it's obviously been in me for a long time.

'When I said that to her, she just said, 'Don't be silly, don't be stupid.' Again, we're talking 20-odd years ago when mental illness, nobody would have known anything about. Nobody would have cared. People just got on with stuff.'

What made you do it in the end?

'I probably had a bit more, I remember having a drink so I was probably braver to get to the stage where you wanted to get to. You talk yourself out of it. It was always in there in my mind, creeping in there, and you're just trying to fight it off.'

How are you still here?

'It got to the stage, I was at a bad stage, trying different medications, there were people from a crisis centre coming to the house every day. Doctors and nurses came every day to check after the second time I done it. After that I felt low. I went to them and said: 'I don't feel good'.

'I went to the doctor with Lucie and I said: 'I just want this pain in my head to go away, I need this feeling to go away, whatever it is inside my head please make it go away'. This was three or four years ago. Lucie was crying her eyes out. She had seen close up what I was going through every day.

'They put me on lots of different medication at the same time. I had blood tests done every week, I was on lithium too but that's also for bulimia, which I didn't realise at the time, so I started putting on weight and at the time I didn't understand. I put on three stone in nine months which, again, doesn't fucking help your moods. I was down to having one small meal a day. I was doing as much exercise as I could, everything I could to lose weight and then I stopped taking tablets last summer overnight when I got back from holiday.'

What happened when you did that?

'The doctor was not happy but I feel alright, I feel grand. I've got to the stage where I have a different outlook on life, on football and all the rest of it. I'm not going to kill myself for this job. I've done it with others. I'm not going to let a job have that impact on me anymore. There is more to life, I've got the girls, Lucie, my family.

'I generally feel in a much better place and in a more relaxed mindset. Probably being quiet and overthinking everything doesn't help. I always sort of go into a lot of detail in my mind of things and why things happen and why things don't happen. I've always been like that. I feel like I carry a lot inside my mind and now I generally don't really worry too much. There is more to fucking life than worrying about every little thing. It's a mindset you're in, you've been as well as you're going to be so anything above that is going to be better isn't it?'

Is your family the reason for that change?

'Lucie is made of strong stuff. Women are generally stronger than men, I think. Knowing that you have her behind you is always good, it makes life easier. Still, it's not nice, it's not fair for her to put her through it. She has been through a lot of shite.

'Other women might have walked away and said they had enough, they don't need it. Some of the stuff I put her through, I wouldn't have got out of bed for four or five days at a time. I wouldn't have eaten, wouldn't have drank. She got to a stage where she just asked: 'What do you want me to do?'

'These moods would come and go and then be quite frequent. She would just ask, 'What do you want me to do? Do you want me to talk to you? Want me to leave you alone?' I didn't know. When I'm in this place I don't want to speak to anyone.

'The door would be closed, she had to get on with life outside that door with the kids. As easy as you go into it, you just as quickly can come out of it. I literally spent days upon days lying on bed doing nothing. That's done now.

'To see B smiling, the little things that make her happy,

that is what keeps you going. Seeing Sadie grow up and Lexie too. I just want to try give my kids the best upbringing possible. Lucie has had to do so much by herself. She really is an amazing woman.'

A few minutes later and the laughing and joking continues. This feels close to understanding how the depths of depression can co-exist side by side with vacuous smiles. Joe Royle, one of the Wigan directors who was appointed by the club's new owners last year, is cracking jokes and telling stories about past glories with Everton.

There are memories of beating Manchester United in the 1995 FA Cup final.

There are stories about Duncan Ferguson.

There are more stories about Duncan Ferguson.

Moore smiles and gets involved in the craic. That's how easy it is to bare your soul in depth and return to the shallow ease of nostalgia.

The road is calling once again.

Blackburn U18s versus Wolves U18s. It is a shorter drive, around 30 minutes, and most of the journey is carried out in silence. Rovers' academy is a minute's drive from the first-team's training centre and is part of a complex that also includes a housing estate that perhaps only footballers could afford to live in.

We sign in for the U18 game and must wear badges citing said fixture. The U16s are playing on a pitch a few yards away but there is a steward ensuring people do not cross over. It is strict.

The game we are watching is also extremely poor. Blackburn take an early lead and the Wolves' players' heads drop. When a second goes in there is no reaction. These games do not illicit many memories for Moore, it is a totally different environment.

'I always come away thinking, 'Do any of these kids have the mindset to be the best player on the pitch?' That was always what I wanted at that age, to be the best on the pitch. I get the feeling some now just want some nice bits for their video clips.

'There are not enough kids wanting to have an effect on games, they're not taking games by the scruff of the neck here, so if they're not going to be the best player here how can they expect to try and be the best in the reserves or get into the first team?

'The lads who do show it, and there are a few, they stand out a mile.'

No one is in this tame encounter, while there is all sorts of excitement coming from the pitch behind us, where a diminutive two-footed midfielder is running the show for Wolves. 'The difference is those lads there will have a nice contract already,' Moore says, pointing to the U18s' pitch. 'The kids over here are playing for one.'

At half-time, former Manchester United U18 manager Paul McGuinness, now the English FA's National Coach Developer, makes a beeline for Moore. There are a raft of young coaches, ranging from clubs as diverse as Premier League champions Manchester City to League One Walsall, here to learn.

The two compare notes on what they have been watching. There isn't much to excite. The small kid running the show for Wolves U16s is taken off at half-time. It later transpires he is from Australia and his family moved to Britain to help him follow his dream.

We leave soon into the second half to go for lunch, the wind is howling and we have a trip across the Pennines for

Leeds-Sheffield Wednesday at Elland Road to contend with. For some of that hour and a quarter we listen to the Championship scores come in.

Millwall and Sheffield United is scoreless.

Rotherham are two-nil down to Stoke.

So far so good for Wigan's survival hopes.

I fall asleep, my head slowly dropping before giving in. Alan laughs when I wake up not far from Leeds.

'You snore worse than the dog.'

'So long as I wasn't drooling like him.'

Elland Road is visible over the horizon on the drive towards the city from the motorway. We pay the £3 for parking and now it's Alan's turn to have a nap, grabbing 30 minutes to himself in the car while I soak up some of the atmosphere around the ground.

A double-decker bus brings scores of visiting supporters. They see me and flick the Vs, banging on the windows and gesturing that I'm a wanker. I'm not a Leeds fan but it seems only right to return the favour.

We collect our complimentary tickets and take our seats right by the away fans. I keep my hands to myself this time. Just prior to kick off, the stadium is given a huge boost by Millwall's late equaliser against their promotion rivals Sheffield United.

That's not good news for Wigan, though, and nor is the fact Rotherham have also levelled with two second-half strikes at Stoke.

Leeds look sluggish and after Keiren Westwood, the occasional Ireland international, makes a couple of impressive saves, nerves begin to grow. They are put to bed when they break the deadlock soon after the break.

Moore has been studying the patterns of play intently, scribbling notes into his small pocket-sized notepad.

He brings up West Brom's Jay Rodriguez as the best player in the division. 'The smartest by a distance, he has a first touch very few defenders can deal with.'

His personal memories of this famous old ground are mostly bad. 'This is where we were relegated with Middlesbrough,' he recalls.

We leave with about 15 minutes to go to avoid getting stuck in traffic. There is one last stop to make before Moore can return home to Lucie and the girls to attend a neighbour's daughter's birthday party.

On the way to dropping me off at a hotel by Leeds Airport, he discusses some of the audio books that have kept him company over the course of this season.

The Subtle Art of Not Giving A Fuck and Chimp Paradox get special mention.

'I'm always curious, always reading why people would say certain things or act in a certain way. Someone like [Marcelo] Bielsa, he is a perfectionist and when you're a perfectionist you're never going to get to the end of what you want to achieve.'

Now I'm worried we might not get to the hotel. The sat nav has taken us off the main roads and into a small housing estate. Eventually we come out the other end of a lane with the hotel in view.

The end of the weekend is here.

Alan helps me with my bags and thanks me for coming.

The next day, Wigan draw with Norwich and a few days later they beat Leeds at Elland Road to effectively confirm safety.

It's the ending he wanted for the story of this season.
His own one continues. Thankfully.

SIXTEEN

A STONES OF A RIDE

—

BRENDAN COFFEY | 12 MARCH

'I'VE LOADS OF BLIND SPOTS,' says Ted Walsh from the comfort of his living room.

'I get angry very easy. I say too much most times. Mouthy. My father was quiet as a mouse. Mother too. I would always be strong enough to voice my opinion.'

Patrick Mullins interrupts, as if sensing the need to provide Walsh a measure of reassurance.

'I think that's what makes Ted good on TV because I respect his opinion and he's not afraid to say what he thinks,' the younger man offers. 'A lot of time on TV and in writing, people say a lot without saying anything. You need someone who is not afraid to give their opinion and he has the experience to back it up.'

At first glance they might not seem like men given to much introspection. Theirs is a macho world in which brave men and women take hard falls and expect to return to the saddle sooner than nature should allow. But these are far from ordinary horsemen.

Among the general public, Walsh is probably best known for his television punditry. In the racing community his status has long been assured as the pre-eminent amateur jockey of his era.

That he went on to train a Grand National winner only cemented his standing in the game.

'Trainers don't retire, they just die,' Walsh told Eamon Dunphy in an interview. Taken at face value those words fog the picture of his profession, suggesting something akin to addiction when really it is an astute and profound description of what it means to lead a vocational life. Regular hours and work time directives do not apply. It is only when trainers have no more living left that they finally stop. A life lived within racing cannot be lived without it.

Walsh has 68 years on the board and if not in the winter of his career is at least feeling the early evening chill. At 29, Patrick Mullins continues to blossom. Son of Willie, the greatest trainer of his, and perhaps any, generation, he has steadily grown in stature, no longer heir apparent and firmly established in his own right as one of the game's leading lights. Regardless of what has been inherited, his record number of winners as an amateur in the saddle puts him in elite company, seizing a mantle previously occupied by Walsh, the man now sitting beside him on the couch.

'It was a bonus for me to be as successful as I was,' says Walsh, reflecting on an amateur career that was the best of his time, and all time, until Mullins arrived on the scene. 'He [Patrick] had a lot more pressure. Willie was champion amateur and a successful trainer. No one expected Patrick to be as good as he is but at the same time if he was a failure, it would have been a bigger thing. It would be said: 'He's not a bit like his father.' Instead he's a superior rider to his dad, in every way. Willie was as good as it gets at that time but he's [Patrick] brought it to another level. Patrick is as disciplined and as professional as you could get as an amateur.'

Such praise does not come lightly. Outspoken and often disliked for it but astute and quick-witted and so much loved for that, Walsh owns a bespoke collection of verdicts, assessments and views, and delivers them on time, every time. Walsh is clearcut and as fluent now with words as he was with Hilly Way over fences. That win in the Champion Chase of 1979 remains the most notable victory of his race-riding career but the man sitting beside him has scrubbed most of his records from the board.

Mullins eclipsed Walsh in July 2018 when notching the 546th winner of a career that may not yet have reached its peak.

'When I see so many of my friends struggling to get the dream that I've been lucky enough to get, it's very easy to see the luck and opportunity,' says Mullins, dismissing the notion of him as an uncommonly self-aware young man. 'It's not a weight on my shoulders but I want to win! I want to win as much as I can. To me, anyone who competes wants to do that.'

Names of those less fortunate than him quickly come to mind. He shares a house with fellow riders Richie Deegan, Brian Hayes and Rachael Blackmore.

'Look at Rachael Blackmore,' he says insistently. 'She didn't suddenly become a good jockey overnight. She's been working at it for so long. I was in a different position in that I got the opportunity much quicker.'

His own narrative is not quite as straightforward as it might seem. He has the racing bloodlines but did not spend every morning of his youth working with black type.

Secondary school took him away from home, to Clongowes Wood College and the company of bluebloods, sons of leaders from the business and political world. Rugby players dominate the list of sporting alumni — Gordon D'Arcy and Rob Kearney most notable — but Mullins is just as worthy. And like his rugby brethren, he has gone to great lengths to achieve success.

'I was in seven-day boarding school [Clongowes] until I was 18 and then I was in college [Maynooth University] five days a week so I was a proper amateur for a long time,' he says. 'When I was 16, 17 and 18 I was only getting to ride out one weekend a month. I used to sneak over to Charlie O'Neill's, four fields left of school, on a Wednesday and a Saturday. Alexander Banquet was in livery over there. Willie always told me I'd probably only get two or three years at this because I was tall. I never really thought that I would be at it for very long.'

Mullins has travelled far and wide to foster his racing education. For whatever reason, in this corner of the equine world, competing stables welcome visiting rivals without compunction.

'Willie and Jackie [Patrick's mother] would always have encouraged me to go to other yards,' says Patrick. 'I like to see other places as well from a training point of view for the future, to see different ways of doing it. We're so busy at home, it's hard to go away for a long period of time. And we're going through such a golden patch now, it would be a pity to go away. I like to go away to some of the flat yards in England like Gosden's and Hammond's. I've gone to Joseph's [O'Brien] here, John Kiely and Gordon's [Elliot]. It's a great sport like that. There are very few sports I'd say that could you do that.'

In soccer, for instance, managers have been upbraided for espionage. In January, Leeds United manager Marcelo Bielsa provoked a furious response from Derby County when the Rams uncovered a spy at their training ground.

'They like one another,' says Walsh, explaining the culture of their game. 'If Gordon's back was against the wall tomorrow morning over something, there's any one of five or six trainers he could ring and say: 'Listen, I've a problem here. What do you think?' Willie would be the same way.'

Says Patrick: 'You cannot be secretive because staff come and go.'

'Fellas know what's happening in a yard,' Walsh confirms. 'If you're doing something wrong in a yard, you cannot do it on your own.'

Warming to the theme, the pair fall into lively conversation.

Mullins: 'You can have an advantage for a while and then everyone catches up. [Martin] Pipe changed the way he trained in England and now everyone does it. He went to interval training, short and sharp. They all used to gallop real long.'

Walsh: 'They say Christy Ring did it in hurling. Instead of running around the pitch, they sprinted across it because that's all you'll ever be doing, he [Ring] reckoned – sprinting to get the ball and hit it. You could jog off from here [Kill] to Johnstown or Naas but if you went flat out you wouldn't get 100 yards.'

Mullins: 'I remember training with a hurling team in college and when we were doing the laps, I was grand at the top but when we were doing the sprints, I was in the middle of the pack.'

Walsh: 'Paddy Mullins was a very successful trainer but

Paddy Mullins had something about him that he could spot a real good horse. There were very few horses that Paddy Mullins had that were good that he didn't get the best out of. I'd say the same thing applies to Willie. I'll see Willie there, he'll arrive at the Curragh with a bunch of horses to work and the plan would be that all horses are going to work but for some reason when one horse gets off the box, he might say: 'That fella could go for a walk today.' Don't ask me what he'd see. That's something you either have or you haven't. He's got that innate ability to spot things that other lads can't spot.'

Mullins: 'It's experience too.'

Walsh: 'Quevega now. He [Willie] minded her and produced her in six Cheltenhams to win. Sometimes gave her one run, sometimes gave her no run. Nothing textbook.'

Mullins: 'Willie trains by eye. You see a lot of places, especially on the flat, there's just a routine because they're more prisoners of time. They have to run at two and three [years old]. Willie sees every horse every morning. He might say we'll do less with him today. There is a routine and routine is very important but he's not afraid to change it on what he sees. 'He looks a bit light,' or, 'a bit cold in his coat,' he [Willie] might say when you ask him. It doesn't always add up. Sometimes he'll say something and you'll go: That's one plus one and the answer is two. The next thing you'll think you see the same thing and you think one plus one is two but it'll end up being two plus one equals three. It's a slightly different equation because maybe he'll say: 'That horse is always light,' or, 'That horse is heavy boned,' or, 'That's how he looks,' or, 'We need to work him harder.' And he's not always right, same as everyone. But he's right more often than not.'

Walsh: 'If you're afraid of getting beat you'll never win because you'll be cautious all the time. You have to be brave.'

Their discussion approaches the final straight but only because Patrick has an appointment elsewhere. They have been running a good gallop from the start, like those great horses they have ridden to victory at Cheltenham. If Ted is always keen, Patrick prefers to settle, ordering his thoughts before making them a matter of public record. As soon as Ted delivers his latest piece of ornate commentary, Patrick fills a gap a lesser mind would not have spotted.

Mullins: 'Willie would say that Ted might do something and six horses away from him, a gap would close and the other lads would be busy blaming themselves but Ted would have done it and no one would know. Willie would always be explaining this to me on how to race ride and how to ride tight, which I think is a very important part, particularly in bumpers, to be able to ride tight. It's as much your job to make it hard for the other fellas. If you're coming up the outside, you're trying to keep everyone tight on the inside. The fella on the inside might be going the shortest way around, which is fine, but he's going to have trouble in running. You're trying to get a clear run and you're trying to keep everyone else tight. When I started off, Nina [Carberry] was a master at it.'

Walsh: 'She's [Carberry] basically trying to take him [Patrick] out of contention. She knows when she's passing that he's a danger and the lads coming down the inside are not aware of anything. They're riding along nonchalantly because that's what most of them do but she can mosey up, she tightens up so that the lads inside her, unawares, close the gap that Patrick was aiming at. That's race riding. When you go by somebody in a race they should know you went by them. No point in giving everybody a chance. It's no different than rugby or any other sport.'

Mullins: 'One of the first things I learned from my father was to know everybody's name because if you do need a bit of room and you just shout at a fella, chances are he won't move. Whereas if I shout, 'Ted, bit of room,' you're more likely to get it. Also then you have to remember you might call in a favour because you might have given a fella a bit of room at a previous meeting. It might be six months later. 'Remember now Listowel there.'

Walsh: 'The same way you'll remember the fella who fucken didn't give you the room!'

Mullins: 'You always need to know who's in front of you, who's beside you, where the fancied ones are, if the lad in front of you might be a lad who's going to get tired. Is the horse going to get tired? You need to be thinking always 100, 200 yards ahead and what's going to change.'

Walsh: 'It's more about a racing brain than it is about anything else. Whether a fella is stylish or neat, that's nice but it really doesn't have any bearing on the result. The result is how you ride in the race. He [Patrick] is a great judge of pace too.'

Mullins: 'I've been very lucky in that I've had coaches. My mother [Jackie] was champion lady amateur and she was second to Aidan O'Brien in that amateur championship. Willie obviously rode and Ruby [Walsh, Ted's son] I'd be able to talk to so I've had coaches who have taught me this. They would come to me after a race and say: 'You did this wrong.' And I could ask them a question: 'Should I have done that?' It's not coaching in a formal sense but I've been surrounded by people who know what they're talking about.'

Walsh: 'I didn't learn as fast as you. I was very moderate for a long time. I learned through watching other fellas. You could give Ruby as big a bollocking as you ever gave a fella and he wouldn't get upset. You'd say to him, 'You gave that a stones of a ride.' He'd never back answer or question it. He'd take it on board. Right up to the present day, I could ring Ruby and say: 'You weren't great there. Well?' He might have a very good reason but you could still say it to him. I'm sure Willie would say the same to him [Patrick]. Even though he's ridden 500 winners I'm sure there's days when he says: 'You didn't fucken shine on him."

Mullins: 'Plenty of them.'

Walsh: 'He's [Patrick] got to take it on board. You could coach a fella all day but if a fella hasn't got it in him...'

Mullins: 'When you respect the person you're getting it from, it's easy take it on board. I'm always amazed looking at other sports. You see Federer or Nadal and they're on about changing coach or golfers working on their swing. You're never too big to learn and take advice.'

Walsh: 'I think nowadays, if a fella is clever enough, there are a lot of videos that you can look at. When I look back on myself, I think it's a pity we didn't have more videos.'

Mullins: 'Video is huge.'

Walsh: 'If you stand in front of the mirror with a pink tie on you and a black shirt and you think you look well — you can't coach him. If he thinks, 'I look smart here.' When he really looks like a clown. The same way with a fella who looks at a

video and says to himself, 'I gave that a good auld ride now.'
A fella should know. My father [Ruby] would go silent and I
knew I was after making a bollocks of it then.'

Mullins: 'Willie is generally the same.'

Walsh: 'We'd leave Listowel and get into the car, I'd be
driving. And when we get to Limerick, I'd say to my father:
'Would you like a cup of tea?'

'No.'

'Now you're gone from Listowel to Limerick and this is
the first few words we've had. Then we'd pull into the petrol
station and I might say, 'Would you like an ice-cream?' 'No.'
We'd drive all the way home, a long drive through all them
towns, and eventually he might say to me: 'Did you think that
race was on today?' If I had left one late or went a mile too
soon. 'Did someone move the winning post?' I'd say, 'No.'
And he'd come back: 'You were in front plenty soon enough
anyway.'

Mullins: 'Willie is quiet. He wouldn't say a lot but if he does,
five minutes later it's done, it's gone. I remember I rode one in
Galway and I got caught wide in the GPT [amateur handicap]
and then I came too late in the bumper. I was driving his car
home. It was silent and then down a dark road I hit a pothole
bang on, like nailed the pothole. 'Pull in! Pull in!' I pulled in,
in the pitch dark on this little, windy road. 'You're after losing
the bumper and the GPT today, you're not going to break my
car. OUT! I'll drive.' I quickly learned to get my own car and
drive racing myself.'

Before the conversation concludes, they pause for reflection.

'I've always been very competitive,' says Mullins. 'First you
want to ride your first winner, then you want to ride out your

claim. Then you're thinking you'd like a Cheltenham winner, a Grade One winner. And when I got to 21, it looked like I was going to be able to keep my weight and do it long term. You're always aiming for the next thing. I obviously have huge opportunity being where I am and I want to make the most of that so that when I retire I can say I made the very most of it. That's driving me.'

Walsh offers a typically frank assessment: 'He's not going to have regrets. He knows he has to deliver too. And he's delivering. He's in a good position but he knows that he has a big responsibility if Willie sticks him up on Douvan or Un de Sceaux. Patrick is aware of everything that's going on right from the bottom of his toes up. He's not floating through life anyway.'

And for all that both men have seen of life, they cannot imagine a better way.

'A lot of my friends from school, they're working in London or Paris or Berlin,' says Mullins. 'I'd love the opportunity in a parallel life to see something different, live in a different city for six months. But I wouldn't swap what I'm doing. I'm hugely lucky to do what I do. Sure we're not working at all.'

'No,' says Walsh.

This, the shortest of his answers; by far, the most telling.

—

SEVENTEEN

PEOPLE YOU'LL NEVER MEET

—

GAVIN COONEY | 21 SEPTEMBER

SO THE FIVE-in-a-row has finally been done.

What does it mean?

* * *

Dublin are outwardly impervious to grand thoughts of legacy or sweeps of history, so let's start by asking what it means for everyone else.

'We're the last hold-outs!' grins Seán Lowry.

Kerry's failure to deny Dublin what was denied them by Lowry's Offaly in the 1982 All-Ireland final means he and his team retain their status as the GAA's most storied renegades.

While that team's place in history is fixed, everything around them has shifted, tilted and irrevocably moved.

'When I was playing, we used to beat Dublin with one hand behind our back', says Lowry.

'This is in the '70s, when I was playing first with Offaly. I remember once beating them by 10 or 12 points, there wasn't a thousand people from Dublin in Croke Park at it.

'GAA wasn't as popular then [in the capital]. You played soccer, followed United and looked up to people like Liam Brady. Then Heffernan began to make it popular and it evolved from there.

'I remember we were playing in the Railway Cup with Leinster one day, and Paddy Cullen was the sub goalkeeper behind Martin Furlong. I've a brother-in-law in Dublin, a Dub through and through. He used to say that they should allow the country people working in Dublin to play for Dublin.

'Paddy said, 'No way — then they'd say they won it for us!"

Times change. Dublin haven't lost a championship game since 2014 and a Leinster opponent haven't finished within a single score of them in seven years.

Maybe Cullen's nightmare is more palatable once-removed.

'Funding comes because of popularity: if you're not popular, sponsors won't line up,' says Lowry.

'It's up to everyone else to raise the bar. Population is an advantage, of course.

'My theory is that an awful lot of country people went up to Dublin to the civil service, married the girl across the office, and they stayed in Dublin.

'The GAA was bred in them. They brought the GAA with them and they set up all these clubs around Dublin. St Jude's, Oliver Plunkett's — first-generation country people set them up and their children are Dubs.

'Ciarán Kilkenny's mother is a Laois woman, the Brogans' mother is from Kerry and their grandfather is from Mayo.

'I honestly think that everything is geared toward Dublin.

'Today, the young people go to Dublin to work, then they

meet someone and buy a house in Templeogue and we are all losing out down the country.'

Lowry now lives on the fringes of Shannonbridge in West Offaly, having moved there to work for the ESB. With stone fortifications either side of a long, narrow bridge across the Shannon, the place was built for enemies other than progress.

The peat-burning power station dominates the skies around Shannonbridge, while uncertain roads punctuated with 'Caution: Steep Verge' signs map a way across boglands to the village.

Shannonbridge is teetering on a verge of its own.

ESB and Bord na Móna have been the area's main employers for decades, albeit beneath the Damoclean reality of the bog's creeping end. Thus Bord na Móna closed 17 bogs last year alone, and have resolved to stop burning peat by 2028.

They tried to mitigate job losses by asking for planning permission to burn biomass along with peat at the Shannon-bridge power station, but were refused. The biomass would have to be imported, and the ESB were told that continuing to burn peat is 'unjustifiable in the current climate change era'.

The station now faces closure and the loss of 380 permanent and seasonal jobs.

Whereas Croke Park can do their bit for the future by banning single-use plastics and earn kudos from all quarters for doing so, the reckoning with what's to come for other parts of the country is a tangled and complex thing.

'The local narrative would be one of loss,' says parish priest Tom Cox, and it's borne out by a crawl through the village.

Bar a couple of heroic hold-outs living off the summer's tourism, the primary school opposite the church is closed and abandoned, declining and becoming enveloped by unruly growth. A butcher shop opposite a garish Supermacs is vacant too, as filthy windows fitfully light cracked tiles and drooping, faded newspaper posters freeze sporting achievements.

And these are only the ghosts that linger - the village has lost a library and the branch of a bank with little trace, and now faces something greater still.

'There has been a sense of apprehension and now the guillotine has fallen,' says Fr Cox.

'As of 1 January it looks like it will be a whole new world.

'But there is a bigger issue than just Shannonbridge: we live in a country in which more than 50% of our GDP is generated in the Greater Dublin Area.'

The world has shifted, albeit not just in response to Dublin's gravity.

'Yeah it's gone and Ferbane is the same, it's beyond rescue,' says Lowry.

'The motor car has a lot to do with it. People have a lot of money now. When they have a bundle of money they go to Athlone to Tesco, Aldi, and Lidl. Growing up we had no option, you went to Ferbane and it kept everything going.

'Time goes on and this is the natural progression.'

In the GAA, time has reached the point at which the five-in-a-row is no longer just something thwarted. Once a barometer beyond greatness, now it has been reached by a side making it look as natural as brushing their teeth in the morning.

Lowry readily admits Dubin are the greatest team to ever play the game, and Jim Gavin would be proud to hear him eschew individual praise in favour of the collective.

'It's probably the team ethic. I think the biggest difference between the two teams was Dublin backed up one another all day long.

'Every time a Dublin player got in trouble, they had someone off their shoulder. Kerry didn't have that. When they got into bother, there was often no one there. Maybe they weren't athletic enough. I don't believe you could get on the Dublin team without being an athlete.

'Being a good footballer isn't good enough anymore. If you're not an 11-second 100-metres man, you can throw your hat at it.'

Did he ever foresee the game demanding as much as it does today?

'Sure you couldn't see that coming. But you'll interview someone in 10 years' time and they'll say the same, at the level it's gone to at that stage.

'We don't know what that will be yet or how it will look, but someone will do something differently.

'It's evolving, and changing all the time.'

Just like everything else.

* * *

We ask what the five-in-a-row means to Dublin as they've never really told us.

They sloughed off all mention of it ahead of the final, with Michael Darragh Macauley telling RTÉ ahead of the drawn game that the number five no longer meant anything to him. A couple of players made reference to it amid the immediate ecstasy of full-time in the replay, and Philly McMahon thrust an open hand to Hill 16 in celebration.

Many others, however, said this would be merely the latest notch on their journey with Dublin and they have no intention of stopping here.

They deliberately filtered out talk of their tilt at history in preparation, and cognisance of success and achievement has always been seen as a self-defeating thing in the Dublin camp.

Before the 2017 final win over Mayo, the dressing-room bore a banner reading 'Success will follow you precisely because you had forgotten to think about it'.

Lowry takes a different approach to Offaly's in '82. He talks with reverence of Michael Foley's book on the final, Kings of September, along with the recent TV documentary, Players of the Faithful.

'I love to see it done, as it is there in the archives for the children's children's children to look back on. Far too often we don't do that, we don't make it until it's too late.'

His side's approach to the media was indicative of a different era, too. Journalist David Walsh was allowed to train with the side the week ahead of the final, while manager Eugene McGee kept a column in the Sunday Tribune throughout the year.

In spite of all of the differences, however, there are similarities between the two teams who find themselves defined by the opposite sides of the five-in-a-row.

Jack McCaffrey spoke to reporters in the team hotel the morning after the All-Ireland success and talked about the future. 'We did a bit of an exercise earlier this year where we paired up and you said to the other lad what you respected in them. I was with Bernard Brogan and I just ended up saying to him: 'In 25 years I can see myself texting you, 'Will we grab lunch?''

'What brings us together is we're decent footballers and playing well together. What I love about this group is that I am really good friends with them and I have a deep, deep love for them.'

Lowry says the bond remains between the '82 team, and they meet up once every five years in September to talk about, around and beyond their legend. He tells a story which may elucidate what the five-in-a-row might mean to a Dublin side outwardly allergic to mythmaking.

In the week leading up to the final in '82, Lowry's aunt passed away. Sitting in his cousin's house after the Mass, a stranger sat beside him and told him that he hadn't begun to realise what he was playing for on Sunday.

The stranger spoke of how he spent his youth crouched with neighbours around a radio listening to Michael O'Hehir paint All-Ireland finals, allowing listeners to worship men they may never see.

'That's what will happen to you on Sunday. You are playing for people who you will never, ever meet.'

The encounter squatted in Lowry's head. 'He looked at it from a different perspective. We were thinking about Offaly supporters. What that got me thinking about was those in America and Australia, those who couldn't come home.

'You can imagine what they would feel like if you did win the All-Ireland. Even though they were thousands of miles away, imagine how they would feel, with their chests out. Imagine what proud Offaly people they would be.'

He sculpted and polished it across the days leading to the final, and tipped off Richie Connor that he had something to say in the dressing room before throw-in. After Eugene McGee had said his bit, Connor counselled further silence as 'Seán Lowry has something he wants to say'.

'Now lads,' began Lowry with practised words but unrehearsed emotion. 'You're not just playing for yourselves today. You're playing for your family and your county and for people you'll never see or meet.

'People from all over the world this weekend, from places

like America, Australia, New Zealand, they'll all have their chest out on Monday if you beat Kerry.

'You'll never see them. There are old people living down small country roads all over Ireland who are rooting for you today, but you'll never meet them and you'll never realise the huge lift you'll give all those people if you go out and beat Kerry today.'

Liam Currams would later tell Lowry he knew Offaly would win from the moment the speech was finished. McGee wrote the same in his book, and years later, phoned Lowry to ask what he had said.

Lowry typed it out and emailed it back.

It was Lowry who held the ball when PJ McGrath blew for full-time to confirm Offaly's ransacking of all sense and expectation. Given only the players were rewarded with medals, Lowry and some of the senior players decided that the football would be McGee's token of history.

Before handing it over, Lowry had it inscribed by Sister John Manning, a Kerry nun working in the primary school in Ferbane. Along with the date and score, she added 'Uíbh Fhailí, Mo Cheol Sibh; Ciarraí, Beidh Lá Eile'.

As the years passed, the ball became a rod for rumour. Some claimed McGee raffled it in support of Matt Connor; several more claimed they knew who had it.

Lowry saw McGee with it only once — at the launch of his autobiography. The ball didn't make an appearance at the 25th anniversary gathering, although McGee told Lowry it would be donated to the Croke Park museum.

Sad circumstances brought Lowry and his team-mates together again in May of this year, at St Mel's Cathedral in Longford for the funeral of Eugene McGee.

As the Mass moved to the presenting of gifts to mark

McGee's life, Lowry's wife Nuala nudged him in the ribs.

'What was the first gift? The ball!'

Later, as the priest moved to his homily in memory of McGee, Lowry was given another nudge.

'The priest began, 'Now lads, you're not just playing for yourselves today. You're playing for your family and your county and for people you'll never see or meet...'

'Then he said, 'That was the speech given by Seán Lowry before Offaly went out onto the field in '82.'

'He gave the full speech.

'I just thought to myself how proud I was. Where would you hear this?

'It's amazing. This is 37 years after the fact, that's what amazes me about it.'

Dublin's place in Ireland and Gaelic football is unlikely to ever recede to the extent Offaly's has, but time will move on for Jim Gavin and his players as it does for everyone else. It's just about the only thing as remorseless as they are.

'I remember talking to the Galway guys from the '70s,' says Lowry. 'They lost the All-Ireland in '71 to Offaly, '73 to Cork and '74 to Dublin, so they won no All-Ireland.

'I asked if they meet up often and one of them said, 'No, we never meet because we never won.'

'Our bond is always there. I still tell young fellas playing finals that this will stick with you for the rest of your life. You will always remember this, you will always cross the road to meet this person, whether it is in 20 or 50 years' time.

'Here I am at 67 years of age, and I vividly remember what happened on fields in county finals and All-Ireland finals.

'It's a fantastic thing.

'You say it's permanent? Yeah, it's permanent.'

The bogs surrounding Seán Lowry in Shannonbridge have always been an easy metaphor for memory and history, but truthfully they have become emblems of a vanishing age and an uncertain, diminished future.

Better to seek life's dignities in sport's permanent glories.

A star in the sky Eoin O'Callaghan (27 JANUARY)
The Fifa Women's World Cup, hosted in the summer of 2019 in France, felt like a watershed moment for the sport.

Anne O'Brien was one of the trailblazers of the women's game, leaving Dublin in the '80s to forge an amazing career in continental Europe's leagues. Despite reaching the sport's pinnacle, her achievements rarely earned headlines at home.

Eoin O'Callaghan spoke to the late player's brother, Tony O'Brien, about Anne's life, career and legacy in this piece which won the inaugural Investec 20x20 award, a prize aimed at recognising coverage of women's sport.

—

About Schmidt Murray Kinsella (23 AUGUST)
Joe Schmidt announced that his massively successful time in charge of Ireland would come to an end with Ireland's Rugby World Cup campaign.

Since arriving in Ireland, the New Zealander has won two European Cups with Leinster and, with the national side, three Six Nations championships. He also masterminded historic wins over the All Blacks, a series victory in Australia and guided the nation to a world ranking of No 1. Murray Kinsella delves into the character that helped make him such a successful coach, in this piece published before he and the Ireland squad flew to Japan for the 2019 tournament.

The hobgoblin of the mediocre mind
Gavin Cooney (23 FEBRUARY)

Eamon Dunphy has been a part of Irish public life for decades. Now, no longer a fixture of the RTÉ football panel with his old friends John Giles and Liam Brady, he allowed Gavin Cooney into his home where they reflected on Dunphy's TV career, his departure from Montrose, regrets and his plans for the future.

—

Half the world away *Sinéad Farrell* (30 MARCH)

Over 53,000 people packed the Adelaide Oval for the climax of the women's professional Aussie Rules season in March. Ailish Considine finished her first year Down Under by starring in the Crows' comprehensive 63-18 win over Carlton.

Drafted as a rookie in 2018, the Clare native kicked a goal to help seal the win for the home side in the league's third season.

—

The champion golfer *Ryan Bailey*

Shane Lowry made his Major breakthrough in memorable circumstances in front of an Irish crowd in the summer of 2019. The Offaly native moved into a share of the 36-hole lead at the Open Championship at Royal Portrush, after successive opening rounds of 67. He then shot a course record 63 to take the outright lead on Saturday night.

Where before he failed to take advantage of a leading position on the Sunday of a Major tournament, this time Lowry won the tournament, and the Claret Jug, by six shots ahead of England's Tommy Fleetwood.

An officer and a GAA manager Kevin O'Brien (28 AUGUST)
Jim Gavin led Dublin to a historic five-in-a-row of senior
All-Ireland victories after a replay win over Kerry in September
on a scoreline of 1-18 to 0-15 points. A brilliant manager,
Gavin served in the Air Corps between 1990 and 2008. Ahead
of the first final meeting with the Kingdom this season, he
opened up to Kevin O'Brien about how his years serving in
the military helped shape his character and outlook. Gavin
now works in the aviation industry.

—

Coffee at the crossroads Sean Farrell (24 MARCH)
What happens afterwards? Michael Allen spoke to Sean Farrell
about dealing with the unexpected and premature end to a
promising sports career. Allen moved from Ulster to Edinburgh
in 2015, where, ultimately, his career wound down. Dealing
with a loss of identity and an income, Allen says the decision
to walk away is the best he's made. He now works in financial
services.

—

Walk of life Paul Fennessy (24 MARCH)
Kate Veale represented Ireland in race walking, claiming gold
at the World Youth Championships in 2011. After various
setbacks, the Waterford athlete is now aiming to make it to
the Tokyo Olympics in 2020. Paul won the Investec 20x20
award for July in recognition of his piece on former Ireland
soccer international Olivia O'Toole.

The old man and the club Fintan O'Toole (16 MARCH)
Donie Sheahan coached East Kerry to the inaugural All-Ireland club championship crown in 1971 and has seen his club Dr Crokes win two since. The 92-year-old headed for Dublin again ahead of the Killarney side's bid to win a third senior national title in March but first looked back on his long association with the game, as well as horse racing and life in the Kingdom through the years with Fintan O'Toole.

Crokes were beaten by Corofin of Galway on a scoreline of 2-16 to 0-10 on St Patrick's Day.

—

Looking down on Leanne Emma Duffy (4 MAY)
Leanne Kiernan ended her first season in English football preparing for an FA Cup final. The Cavan native moved from Shelbourne to West Ham in 2018 and quickly settled into London life. The Ireland international's family spoke to Emma Duffy about Leanne's love of the game, the loss of her brother and supporting her from afar. The Hammers ultimately lost the Wembley showpiece to Manchester City, 3-0.

Emma's feature on Irish footballer Isibeal Atkinson was named the winner of the April 20x20 award.

—

Lord and Master Ryan Bailey (15 JULY)
Dubliner Eoin Morgan captained England to a dramatic Cricket World Cup victory on home soil in July. A batsman, he previously played for Ireland and now lines out for county side Middlesex. England became world champions for the first

time, beating New Zealand in the final on boundaries after the match and super over were tied.

—

The rocky road Aaron Gallagher (11 MAY)
Christy McElligott played in the League of Ireland, with Brian Kerr's title-winning St Patrick's Athletic amongst others, and with the Ireland Junior side before he lost a leg in a road traffic accident in 2000.

The Ballymun native was one of the founding members of the Irish Amputee Football Association. He has caps for the national side, has been a driving force behind the league and has now set his sights on coaching. This piece was named Best Feature at the FAI Communications Awards.

—

After the Garden Gavan Casey (4 JUNE)
Katie Taylor defeated Delfine Persoon in Madison Square Garden in the summer of 2019 in a controversial split decision. Following her victory in New York, however, she became one of only seven boxers in history, female or male, to hold all four major world titles.

The Bray native is scheduled, at the time of writing, to headline the Manchester Arena in November in another career landmark.

Keeper of the faith Paul Dollery (31 DECEMBER)
Though he didn't start the season as first-choice goalkeeper for
St Finbarr's senior football side, John Kerins Jr found himself
between the posts for the Cork club's championship decider
against Duhallow at Páirc Uí Chaoimh in October 2018.

Kerins' father was the intercounty netminder in the No 1
jersey for the Barr's the last time they won the county championship in 1985.

—

Living the dream, surviving the pain David Sneyd (25 MAY)
David Sneyd spent a weekend with former Ireland international Alan Moore towards the end of the cross-channel
football season. As they buzzed between Moore's family
home in Yorkshire, his work at football grounds in the north
of England and the pub, the pair discussed the Dubliner's
Premier League heyday in teams with Juninho and Ravenelli,
depression, recovery and more.

—

A stones of a ride Brendan Coffey (31 DECEMBER)
Ted Walsh is the patriarch of the best-known Irish racing
family. A much-loved and respected voice in TV and radio
coverage, he's communicated, in his unique style, a passion and
knowledge of the sport for decades. He was also a successful
amateur jockey and, later, trainer with Papillion winning the
Grand National in 2000 and Commanche Court the Irish
Grand National in the same year; both were ridden by his

son, Ruby.

Patrick Mullins is a successful amateur jockey. He's the son of renowned trainer Willie Mullins and Jackie, a former successful amateur rider.

Brendan Coffey won the 20x20 monthly award for May for a piece on *The42* about racing driver Nicole Drought.

—

People you'll never meet *Gavin Cooney* (21 SEPTEMBER)
Seán Lowry was a key part of the Offaly team that denied Kerry a famous five-in-a-row of All-Irelands with their football championship win in 1982. Hours after Dublin became the first side to achieve that record, Gavin Cooney met with Lowry to ask what the win means for him and his former teammates, what it says about Dublin and, ultimately, what Dublin's dominance tells us about the GAA and Ireland.

ACKNOWLEDGEMENTS

IF DONNCHA O'CALLAGHAN was the man forever lauded for doing the 'unseen work' on the rugby pitch, it takes a whole squad of his kind to bring a book like this to fruition. To each and every person involved in this, the third volume of what has become our annual Behind the Lines anthology, a sincere thanks.

Firstly, to the people who have featured within these pages and elsewhere on *The42* this year. Thank you for your openness and honesty in sharing your stories, and for allowing us to bring them to a wider audience.

Our thanks as well to all who have signed up to *The42* Membership following its launch this summer, not only for your ongoing backing, but for your valuable feedback in helping us to shape the direction of this year's Behind the Lines cover; we hope you like the finished product, once again nurtured from concept to design and execution by Graham Thew.

Journal Media CEO Adrián Acosta was the man who drove us to dip our toe into the world of book publishing with Behind the Lines Volume 1 back in 2017. Once again, he encouraged us to be ambitious — as in everything — and then was generous with his time and energy to make sure that we had the support we needed.

Our brilliant colleagues across the various constituent parts in Journal Media have always been supportive with their feedback and help, in too many different forms to list here. Thank you in particular to Sinéad Casey, who looked after so many of the vital publishing logistics while we experimented with chapter order and cover colours. Thanks also to Kara Browning, Susan Daly, Paul Kenny, and to Brian and Eamonn Fallon.

We are always grateful to Sinéad O'Carroll who, somehow, found the time once again to bring her editorial expertise to bear on the early drafts of the manuscript and point us in the right direction. Thanks to both Paul Dollery and David Sneyd who brought their scalpels to the final copy-edit before we hit print.

And finally to you, our readers, for buying this book and once again supporting our work. Many of you have been with us since our early days as *TheScore.ie*, and as we prepare to celebrate our 10th birthday in 2020, our commitment to produce the great journalism and quality storytelling that you want to read is as strong as ever. This whole show couldn't, and wouldn't, happen without your support. Thank you.

NIALL KELLY
Deputy Editor, The42